Issues in Education
GENERAL EDITOR: PHILIP HILLS

The Quiet Child

Other books in this series

Michael Barber: *Education and the Teacher Unions*

Gordon Batho: *Political Issues in Education*

David Bosworth: *Open Learning*

John Darling and Anthony Glendinning: *Gender Matters in Schools*

Norman Evans: *Experiential Learning for All*

Paul Fisher: *Education 2000*

Leo Hendry, Janet Shucksmith and Kate Philip: *Educating for Health*

Eric Hoyle and Peter D. John: *Professional Knowledge and Professional Practice*

Roy Todd: *Education in a Multicultural Society*

Geoffrey Walford: *Choice and Equity in Education*

Michael Williams: *In-service Education and Training*

Janet Collins

The Quiet Child

CASSELL

Cassell
Wellington House
125 Strand
London WC2R 0BB

127 West 24th Street
New York
NY 10011

First published 1996

British Library Cataloguing-in-Publication Data
A catalogue record for this book is available from the
British Library.

ISBN 0-304-33472-3 (hb)
    0-304-33473-1 (pb)

Typeset by Action Typesetting Ltd, Gloucester

Printed and bound in Great Britain
by Biddles Ltd, Guildford and King's Lynn

Contents

Foreword: the purpose of this series

The educational scene is changing rapidly. This change is being caused by a complexity of factors which includes a re-examination of present educational provision against a background of changing social and economic policies, new forms of testing and assessment, the National Curriculum, local management of schools involving greater participation by parents, and the various recent Education Reports.

As the educational process is concerned with every aspect of our lives and our society both now and for the future, it is of vital importance that all teachers, teachers in training, administrators and educational policy-makers should be aware of and informed on current issues in education.

This series of books is thus designed to inform on current issues, look at emerging ones, and to give an authoritative overview which will be of immense help to all those involved in the education process.

Philip Hills
Cambridge

Acknowledgements

This book and the research on which it is based could not have been written without the help of a large number of people. Acknowledgement is offered with gratitude to those many pupils, teachers and tutors who have helped to shape my thinking. I owe special thanks to Bernard Harrison. He has been a constant source of encouragement throughout the long, and at times difficult, process. Thanks are also due to the many friends and research colleagues at Sheffield University, Leeds University and The Open University whose encouragement and advice have stimulated and sustained me. I am also grateful to Sheffield University for awarding me a studentship to fund the research.

For their comments on early drafts of this book I am extremely grateful to Lyn Dawes, Neil Mercer and Joan Swann. Their advice has been invaluable. For other extremely constructive conversations I thank Kathy Mayoh, Peter Scrimshaw, Ruth Townsley and Jo Weinberger. For their constant friendship and support I would like to thank Anne-Marie Barron, Janet Coles, Carol Dale, Sharon Goodman and Veronica Wigley. My gratitude to Terry goes too deep for words. My final, but probably most important, thanks go to the families who allowed me into their lives. I remember them with more than mere affection.

1 Introduction

What is required is not more of the same. If we are to reach the unreached and include the excluded, more must mean different.
Report of the Rome Lifelong Learning Conference, 1994

This book grew out of a growing frustration at my inability to communicate with, and therefore teach, a group of quiet withdrawn pupils who seemed unable or unwilling to join in the social and academic conversations of my class. My problems were twofold. First, these pupils exhibited behaviour which discouraged communication. They rarely spoke in class and seemed reluctant to ask for help even when they were experiencing difficulties with their work. During discussions they were unenthusiastic and seemed unable or unwilling to engage with others. Their body language and lack of eye contact inhibited conversation. They adopted a passive role, which meant that, whilst they would answer questions, often giving monosyllabic answers, they hardly ever initiated discussion or asked questions. These pupils tended to be social isolates spending a great deal of time alone. Their lack of friends in the class meant that it was difficult for them to find partners or to work with their peers during group activities.

My second problem was that of trying to hear and respond to the pupils' silence in a room full of noise. Working as I did in an inner city school with a high proportion of loud, potentially aggressive pupils, it was often difficult to notice the quiet ones. These quiet and compliant pupils did not present discipline problems; on the contrary, I was aware that I was guilty of appearing to condone their quiet behaviour by sometimes ignoring them in my anxiety to cope with the demands made by other, potentially disruptive pupils. Even when I was aware of the needs of quiet pupils it was still extremely difficult to find the time and energy to really get to know them.

I knew that the quiet pupils' compliance did not necessarily equate with a commitment to learning. I suspected that these pupils were 'playing truant in mind whilst present in body, [seeing] neither the relevance nor the reason for all they are asked to do' (Young, 1984, p. 12). Although they completed the bare minimum of work, they appeared to have little interest or investment in the outcome. 'They conform, and even play the system, but many do not allow the knowledge presented to them to make any deep impact upon their view of reality' (Barnes, 1979, p. 17).

My concern for the quiet pupils stemmed from beliefs about the importance of talk for learning. I knew talk was central to children's cognitive and emotional development and that children developed their perception of themselves and their world through talk. Language, and particularly spoken language, is the way in which 'successive generations of a society benefit from the experience of the past, and it is also language that each new generation uses to share, dispute and define its own experience' (Mercer, 1995, p. 4).

Talk is particularly important in schools, especially at primary school level when pupils are just beginning to learn to read and write. In these situations talk is the main medium of instruction and assessment. By talking to children and listening to what they have to say teachers assess and support children's learning. For pupils to be successful and make the most of the learning opportunities offered it is important that they become active participants in the discourse of the classroom.

Despite my best efforts, attempts to encourage quiet pupils to participate in discussions had little effect. This was particularly true in whole-class or large-group discussions. Quiet pupils rarely volunteered answers and when they did they invariably put up their hand just as I chose other pupils. Choosing quiet children who did not have their hand up seldom succeeded and was likely to increase both the pupil's obvious discomfort and my frustration at their lack of involvement. Teachers of quiet children will understand the dilemma. Allowing children to be passive observers deprives them of important learning experiences, but these pupils appear to be so nervous that even the gentlest persuasion seems like a violation. The lesson which I describe below illustrates this point very well.

Hearing silence in a room full of noise

It was the autumn term, and the school was invited to participate in a City Council initiative to clean up the local environment. Given that the request came during a week already designated as 'poetry week', I decided that my class of eight-year-olds would contribute a book of poems about litter. In order to ensure that all the children had something to contribute to the lesson and to develop 'common knowledge' within the class, I presented the class with a series of stimuli. We looked at a set of slides about litter provided by the Council. We also surveyed the school grounds in order to identify the areas where litter had accumulated. After the 'clean-up campaign' we would revisit these sites to assess the improvements. Although the children would ultimately be responsible for writing their own poems, I chose to begin with a collaborative activity. I believed that collaboration on a first draft of the poem would help to motivate the less able by providing them with an opportunity to express themselves orally and on equal terms with their more able peers. I hoped that the process of contributing to a group poem would ensure success for all pupils.

The whole class gathered round the blackboard at the front of the class. I provided the class with a possible structure for the poem and brainstorming led to a flood of ideas, words and phrases.

Ryan:	Nappies
Lee:	Bed mattress
Jason:	There is a bed mattress in our park that someone has just left there.
Leonie:	Old clothes
Alison:	Bike wheels
Selina:	Litter, Litter,
	Rats, Cats,
	Cardboard boxes, Bed mattress,
	Old clothes, Bike wheels.
	Litter, Litter
Jason:	We need to swap some of the words round because they are not rhyming.
John:	Why should it be?

I assumed from the rapid flow of ideas that the class were motivated by the task and that the lesson was successful. I was particularly delighted to see the class working together in harmony without the petty squabbles and arguments which characterized many of my earlier attempts at collaborative writing. At least for the moment the class seemed united by a joint purpose. However, the fact that the more vocal pupils were gainfully employed gave me the opportunity to notice Mandy's lack of participation.

Mandy sat still and quiet in the middle of the group. We were half-way through the activity and she had not spoken at all either to make suggestions of her own or to comment on other people's contributions. She stared at the floor, which prevented me from using eye contact to include her in the discussion. Moreover, when I invited her to say something she blushed with embarrassment and did not speak. The class waited. I wanted to give Mandy time to respond but I knew I could not wait long or the class would get restive. Reluctantly, I left Mandy to her silence and continued working with the rest of the class.

For me this lesson highlighted the way in which teachers have, by necessity, to put the needs of potentially unruly children first. It is only when these children are settled that the teacher can devote time and attention to the needs of quiet withdrawn children. Would I have noticed Mandy's passivity if the class had not been so highly motivated? I am ashamed to say probably not. Even once I had noticed Mandy's quiet withdrawn behaviour I was unable to talk with her until the rest of the class had settled down to write their own poems. As soon as I was able, I approached Mandy's desk. She sat with her paper and pencil ready but had not begun to write. Thinking that she was suffering from writer's block I suggested that she could begin by copying the first verse from the board. However, her response indicated her lack of involvement with the task. 'Miss,' she said, 'you know the poem on the board? Who wrote it? Where has it come from?'

I tried to explain that the poem had been written by the class as a collaborative group effort and I identified the contributions made by individual pupils. I was shocked that, despite sitting through the whole process, Mandy had somehow completely missed the point of the activity. Despite her physical presence in the centre of the group she had been totally unaware of the collaborative writing going on around her. In a real sense she was excluded from the group that produced the poem.

This incident and others like it made me realize that my sympathy for Mandy's obvious embarrassment prevented me from developing teaching strategies which would empower her to find a voice in the classroom. Moreover, this was potentially the only area of the curriculum in which I allowed pupils to opt out of an activity. In all other subjects I had devised a number of strategies and teaching materials to support those who lacked confidence or ability. In maths, for example, pupils were encouraged to develop at their own level through a carefully graded individualized maths scheme. Similarly, the book corner contained a range of fiction and non-fiction books to meet a wide range of interests and abilities. Even in practical subjects like PE or design and technology, I presented children with open-ended tasks to ensure that all pupils could respond at their own level. Child-centred activities designed to meet the specific needs of individual pupils were at the centre of all my teaching except, I now realized, in one vital area – the development of spoken language. When it came to developing talk I was not meeting the needs of quiet withdrawn pupils. Moreover, my feelings of dissatisfaction are mirrored in a body of research which is critical of the quality of a lot of the talk which takes place in schools between teachers and pupils.

The quality of pupil–teacher talk

Since the 1970s a number of researchers (see for example, Barnes, 1979; Tizard and Hughes, 1984; Cazden, 1988) have found that, although it was the pupils who were supposed to be the ones doing the learning, they rarely spoke in school except in monosyllables. It was the teacher who had total control of the material to be learned. This is 'controlling not just negatively, as a traffic policeman does to avoid collisions, but also positively, to enhance the purposes of education' (Cazden, 1988, p. 3). Since teachers control the learning in classrooms many discussions are, in reality, a process whereby pupils are led along a predetermined route towards the teacher's preconceived definition of reality. Success is then measured by pupils' abilities to guess what the teacher is thinking and to respond in a way which most closely represents the teacher's answer. Pupils who do not offer what the teacher deems to be the correct formulation of the answer are likely to have their answer rejected or amended by the teacher. Cazden found that a three-part sequence of initiation, pupil response, teacher evaluation (IRE) was the most common pattern of discourse at all levels of compulsory education. This approach was so pervasive that teachers evaluated statements even when the children were the real experts (for example, when talking about their parents' birth place). IRE has become so much a part of school 'culture' that it is accepted by teachers and pupils alike.

In commenting on the nature of teacher-directed talk it is interesting to be reminded of the largely universal rules of such discussions:

Teachers decide who will speak and for how long.

Teachers plan and run the system by which those who wish to speak can have the opportunity to do so. This is usually the 'hands-up' system, although teachers have the power to bypass this, for instance by asking children without their hands up.

Teachers have the final say over the acceptability of particular contributions. They can indicate their approval, or lack of it, verbally or non-verbally.

Teachers can alter any of the rules at their discretion. They may, for instance, allow greater freedom of talking in certain lessons (e.g. art), or on certain occasions (e.g. discussion times).

(Wray and Medwell, 1991, pp. 13–14)

Interestingly, whilst pupils are encouraged to put their hands up, many of the ground rules are not made explicit. For example, I can think of a number of instances when teachers have told children to 'work in silence' but have meant with a 'minimum of noise'. This can lead to confusion and demonstrates another area in which children have to 'guess what the teacher is thinking'. My experience of working with quiet children would suggest that these pupils lack either the skills or the confidence to participate in these kinds of guessing games. Moreover, when talk occurs in public and highly competitive 'whole-class discussions' quiet pupils are unlikely to compete for the teacher's attention.

Sadly, there is evidence to suggest that pupils are denied the opportunity to ask questions and become active participants in their learning from the moment they begin their formal education. In a comparison of children's conversations at home and at school, Tizard and Hughes (1984) observed 30 four-year-old girls, at home with their mothers and during their mornings at nursery school, and noted that

Of those questions that were asked at school, a much smaller proportion were 'curiosity' questions and 'Why' questions, and a much larger proportion were 'business' questions, of the 'Where is the glue?' type, than was the case at home. 'Challenges' were very rare at school, and 'passages of intellectual search' were entirely absent. (Tizard and Hughes, 1984, p. 20)

Of this sample, nearly half of the children asked five questions or less during two mornings at school, and a further three children asked no questions at all. All the girls asked more questions at home than they did at school. Even children young enough to attend nursery school seemed to accept that their role was to answer rather than ask questions. At school they assumed a passive role and were unable or unwilling to enter into the kind of inquisitive dialogue which typified their talk with their mothers at home. It is as if they abandoned their natural curiosity at the school gates.

Small-group work

The limitations of teacher-directed whole-class discussions could be seen as one of the major factors in my failure to communicate with quiet pupils. However, my attempts to create small-group activities were not necessarily more effective. The main difficulty was that in the years that they had been together as a class some children had formed strong friendships which excluded other pupils. Moreover, this particular class, which contained several potentially aggressive pupils, was particularly resistant to co-operative group work.

The nature of the class meant that I experienced great difficulties in trying to organize the class into small groups. I tried a number of different groupings but could not find a way of ensuring that all pupils had a partner with whom they could work well. When I put quiet pupils together there was little talk within the group and they found feedback sessions difficult without someone to speak out for them. When more confident pupils were put together they were often quite critical of each other and wanted me to act as arbiter in their disputes. There was also a danger that asking quiet pupils to work with their more confident peers might lead to the quiet pupils being dominated.

Allowing pupils to choose their own partners was not the solution. Whilst the popular children could select partners from the whole class, other, more reserved or less popular, children often found it difficult to find a partner. A small minority of children were rejected by their peers, who refused to have them in their group. This rejection was often non-verbal with pupils moving away or pulling faces. Perhaps because they feared this type of rejection, a couple of pupils would refuse to participate altogether, saying that they preferred to work alone.

Quiet behaviour is detrimental to learning

As the above accounts demonstrate, quiet pupils are unlikely to be active participants in the discourse of the classroom. They are extremely embarrassed by any attempts to persuade them to talk with teachers or peers. In addition to being a source of embarrassment, quiet non-participatory behaviour is also detrimental to learning. Such behaviour:

- prevents children from learning to express themselves (learning to talk);
- prevents children from asking questions and making the learning their own (learning through talk);
- prevents children from an active exploration of the subject being learned;
- prevents teachers from finding out what children know and thus monitoring and supporting learning;
- reinforces stereotypes (Girls, especially those with moderate learning difficulties, are more likely to exhibit quiet passive behaviour in the classroom than other groups of children.);
- renders children invisible and can reinforce poor self-image;
- can be linked with social isolation and can make pupils vulnerable to bullying;
- can, in a minority of cases, mask serious emotional trauma such as bereavement, abuse, family separation, etc.

A desire to empower these quiet pupils to be active participants in classroom talk led me to begin a four-year research project. An account of this research forms the basis of this book and had two major and related aims: first, to identify the possible causes of the quiet, withdrawn and non-participatory behaviour I witnessed in schools; second, to devise and implement teaching strategies which help to empower quiet pupils to play a more active role in their own education. Before going on to give an account of my research it is appropriate to begin by explaining more about the research and the quiet children who were at the centre of it.

Introducing the research

The first aim of the research was to understand the possible causes of the quiet behaviour I witnessed in my classroom. In particular I wanted to understand the quiet pupils' own perceptions of their experiences. Consequently, it was appropriate to work towards in-depth case studies of the twelve quiet children in my own classroom. These case studies were based on a series of semi-structured interviews with pupils which took place over a three-year period. Issues raised during these interviews were considered alongside data gathered from other sources, such as classroom observations in the pupils' primary and secondary schools, as well as interviews with parents and teachers.

Issues raised during interviews with pupils, their parents and teachers form the basis of Parts One and Two of this book. Part One focuses on the pupils and their experiences of school. Part Two focuses on the pupils' relationships with their parents and the way in which these relationships influence the pupils' perceptions of themselves and their behaviour in school. Part Two also explores the way in which children's early experiences of relationships with parents establish a pattern for subsequent relationships in school.

The second aim of the research was to devise and implement teaching strategies which would be useful in empowering quiet pupils. My experience of implementing such strategies forms the basis of Part Three. I used observations of pupils working in their mainstream classrooms to assess the effectiveness of a range of teaching strategies. My own teaching of the quiet pupils in withdrawal groups and in whole-class situations provided evidence of the strategies I devised.

Researching my own classroom

As my research grew out of observations of a specific group of pupils in my own class, it seemed appropriate that the research should focus on them. Consequently, I began in the small inner city middle school where I had worked as class teacher and language development post-holder during the previous four years.

The fact that I was known in the school and in the local community brought significant advantages which, I would argue, far outweighed any disadvantages I might experience in researching in a familiar setting. The main advantage was that I had already established a good relationship with both the pupils and their parents. I felt that research with quiet withdrawn pupils would be more effective if such work grew out of existing relationships. Although the majority of the pupils had known me for two years before the study began, it still took a long time for some of them to trust and confide in me.

Similarly, I feel that because I was already known and trusted in the local community it was easier for parents to welcome me into their homes and their lives. Certainly, an analysis of the range of issues raised by some parents during the one-to-one interviews suggests that our previous relationship did not prevent them from being honest. Some parents criticized their children's school and the quality of the education they received. Others expressed blatantly racist comments which, they admitted, they were unlikely to repeat in school.

In addition, the fact that I had taught the pupils before was an important prerequisite to being able to carry out the whole-class teaching during the second phase of the study. Experience of supply teaching in the same school demonstrated to me some of the difficulties which an experienced teacher can face when working with a group of children for the first time. I felt that the class which featured in the study would have been less receptive if I had not already established a relationship with them.

The potential difficulties of being an 'inside' researcher were outlined by Judith Bell (1987, p. 45) when describing the experiences of a research student: 'The close contact with the institution and colleagues made objectivity difficult to attain and, he felt, gaining confidential knowledge had the potential for affecting his relationships with colleagues.' I was not trying to achieve 'objectivity' but – to invoke a term from phenomenological enquiry – a 'proper subjectivity'. (This term, in accepting that there is nothing ultimately to be known 'as fact' about the realized world, helps to remind us that knowledge is a matter of inter-relations between the person, the onlooker and the world.) Nevertheless, I do identify with the difficulties associated with trying to carry out research in a school where I had previously worked as a teacher.

The setting

When I began the school at the centre of my research was a middle school for 8- to 12-year-olds, with an annual intake of less than sixty pupils. It was situated in the middle of an inner city area and was housed in half of a large 1920s building which had originally been a secondary modern school. The area had a high level of unemployment and the majority of the pupils lived in rented houses or maisonettes.

The school drew its intake from a multi-ethnic catchment area in which fifty per cent of the population were black, the majority of those being of African–Caribbean origin. The remainder of the black families originated from the Asian subcontinent although the majority of pupils attending the school were born in Britain. Through involvement in the research I learned about a level of racial disharmony in the area of which I had not been aware during the period of my teaching at the school. In addition to racial tensions between the black and white sectors of the community there were also similar conflicts between African–Caribbean and Asian families. Whilst the school worked hard at fostering understanding and tolerance between races, the pupils lived in a world in which racial disharmony was rife. The area around the school was known, by the community and by the police, to be inhabited by a number of drug dealers. During my work with the quiet pupils I was alarmed by the pupils' knowledge of drug abuse and related crimes.

Introducing the pupils

At the beginning of my work the quiet pupils were in the same Year 6 class and all were approaching their eleventh birthday. I worked with them during their last two years at primary school and their first year at secondary school.

The fact that I was researching former pupils meant that I knew the pupils extremely well. As a consequence, the decision as to which pupils should be included in the study was based on first-hand knowledge of how those pupils had behaved whilst I had been their class teacher. Subsequent observations of the selected pupils working with other teachers, both in primary and secondary schools, confirmed that these pupils were likely to exhibit quiet withdrawn behaviour with other teachers and in a range of settings. Thus observations carried out during the course of the study have confirmed my view that the pupils' quiet behaviour was habitual and not merely a response to my own teaching.

Being quiet and withdrawn in class was the one criterion which united the group of selected pupils. In many other respects the pupils were extremely diverse. Ten of the twelve selected pupils were girls, which raised the issue of a possible link between quiet compliant behaviour and gender. During the early days of this research an exploration of the connection between gender and language nearly led to the writing of a completely different book, one which would have focused exclusively on girls and their acquisition of language. However, a recognition of the difficulties which quiet boys experience when they do not conform to a stereotypical view of 'male behaviour', was sufficient to ensure that I worked with both boys and girls. The two boys, Duncan and Pete, lived with their parents and older siblings. Mandy, Roxana and Pamela also lived with both parents and had siblings much older than themselves.

In terms of racial origins the group was mixed. Two pupils, Aberash and Justina, were of African–Caribbean origin, whilst Charlene was of mixed race with a black father and a white mother; Rasheeda was the only Asian pupil to be included in my research. Both Diana and Susie lived with their fathers and younger sisters. However, they differed considerably in their responses to their mothers leaving the family home. Whilst Diana was in regular contact with her mother and accepted the family break-up, Susie had a tempestuous relationship with her mother and found it difficult to accept that they were not going to live together as a family again. She found it hard to adjust to being part of an extended family when her father's girlfriend moved in with her own children. Of the twelve children who participated in the research, Vicky was without doubt the most quiet and withdrawn. Throughout the research she spoke little, even during our one-to-one conversations. Her family saw her quietness as a temporary phase and assumed she would grow out of it.

During the three years of data collection, and despite the fact that the pupils transferred from one primary school to seven secondary schools, I was able to maintain contact with ten of the twelve pupils and their families. It is perhaps indicative of the relationship between Charlene's family and the school that I was unable to obtain an interview with members of her family. I lost contact with Charlene altogether during the second year of the research when, after a period of intermittent truanting, Charlene and her family 'disappeared' from the area without leaving a forwarding address. Similarly, although I maintained contact with Rasheeda's family throughout the research, I lost contact with Rasheeda when she left the city to attend a secondary school near her father. However, I was able to maintain contact with the remaining ten children who took part in all aspects of the study. My relationship with some of those pupils became extremely close and I was pleased that some of them kept in contact with me long after the research finished.

The structure of the book

Part One: The pupils

Chapter Two describes the characteristics of quiet withdrawn pupils and is based on extensive interviews with them. Chapter Three provides an account of four types of quiet withdrawn behaviour. Together these two chapters should help teachers, and parents, to identify and prevent non-particip-atory behaviour in the classroom. Chapter Four draws on special-needs literature and argues that recognizing the special educational needs of quiet withdrawn pupils is an important precursor to empowering them to play a more active role in the social and academic discourses of the class-room.

Part Two: The parents

Having thus established that habitually quiet behaviour is detrimental to learning, Part Two focuses on the connection between parent–child relationships and the quiet behaviour witnessed in schools. Psychologists have long recognized the importance of parent–child relationships in the psychological and emotional development of children. Indeed, my research draws extensively on developments in the area of 'attachment theory' which was first postulated by John Bowlby in the 1960s. Although his work was innovative at the time, it is now widely accepted that anxious attachments in early childhood can distort psychological and emotional development. I believe it is now timely to review the work of Bowlby and others in the light of post-feminist initiatives in this area. Meanwhile, educationalists have been slow to acknowledge the effects of anxious attachments on the learning experiences of children in school, and to apply the research findings to the classroom. Part Two considers the implications of 'attachment theory' on teacher–pupil relationships in school. It concludes with three illustrative case studies.

Part Three: The teachers

Part Three offers an account of teaching strategies which have proven useful in empowering quiet pupils to play an active part in their own education. Amongst these strategies are co-operative small-group work, the use of 'talk partners' and counselling techniques. The merits of personal and social education in building self-confidence and thus empowering quiet withdrawn pupils is also discussed. Chapter Eight describes my work with pupils in withdrawal groups, whilst Chapter Nine focuses on work with quiet pupils in whole-class situations. Chapter Ten examines the importance of one-to-one conversations with quiet pupils and makes recommendations as to how teachers might adopt such an approach. This chapter also identifies the need to provide appropriate professional support for pupils whose silence is a response to acute distress or abuse. Chapter Eleven explores the ways in which giving pupils a voice in the classroom can raise issues which teachers might find difficult or contentious. In this chapter I argue that it is important for teachers to be prepared to talk about issues which are important to pupils and their parents.

Part One
The Pupils

2 Characteristics of habitually quiet pupils

In the context of this book, quiet pupils are described as being those who are unable or unwilling to communicate freely with teachers or peers in school. Indeed, by their own admission, they experience acute anxieties about talking in school, especially in front of large groups of relative strangers. Their reluctance to talk seems, at least in the school context, to be habitual. Quiet pupils do not exhibit a wide repertoire of behaviour. It is as if they do not have access to a wide variety of responses, as if they have no choice.

Related to their anxieties about talking, quiet pupils also have difficulty in forming and sustaining relationships with peers and have poor relationships with teachers in school. Drawing on illustrative case studies, this chapter examines each of these characteristics in turn and suggests ways in which schools might support quiet pupils and empower them to take a more active role in their education.

The term 'quiet pupils' implies that they are a homogeneous group. However, as was demonstrated in Chapter One, a limited repertoire of response is, at least on the surface, the only thing these children have in common. They come from a wide variety of ethnic and cultural groups. Moreover, whilst quiet or passive behaviour may be more common amongst girls, this is by no means an exclusively female trait. Quiet pupils also experience a variety of patterns of parenting. Some quiet pupils have experience of parental separation and divorce, whilst others have both natural parents living at home. Consequently, whilst gender, race and home background may prove to be contributory factors they are not themselves predictors of behaviour. An individual's pattern of behaviour is a unique response to a specific set of circumstances.

Anxiety about talking

Generally speaking, quiet pupils are likely to be more talkative at home and with people that they know well.

Mandy: No, I'm not shy at home ... 'cos I know people ... I know all the people at home ... don't know all the people at school.

They tend to be shy when they are being watched by others and their shyness is particularly acute when they are asked to speak in front of the class or during assemblies. Their anxiety about talking in front of others is clearly a disadvantage in whole-class discussions.

For quiet pupils, shyness is associated with a lack of confidence, or anxiety. Aberash acknowledged that whilst being shy was 'normal' it was also extremely frightening: 'You get scared out of your wits'. Moreover, because of the physical symptoms which may be associated with shyness, such as blushing, giggling, looking away or fidgeting, pupils often find it difficult to conceal their anxiety. Knowing that they are likely to blush or giggle can of course make quiet pupils even more self-conscious. Far from being comfortable with their quiet behaviour, these individuals are acutely aware that quiet or shy behaviour can be a handicap in social circumstances.

Justina: 'Cos when you're shy, you're left out of things and you don't get ... get to know ... more people. [My mother] thinks I'm ... ignorant but I'm not ... I can't ... I'm shy to mix with those people.

Thus quiet pupils are aware that their anxiety limits their social lives and makes them appear ignorant or stupid. They may be angry at adults', especially their parents', seeming lack of sympathy for their feelings. The pupils are also aware that they have few strategies for dealing with difficult social situations and are frustrated with themselves for not being able to overcome their shyness. Consequently, whilst they may wish to change their behaviour they simply do not know how. It is as if they are locked into 'extreme and rigid' modes of behaviour. Such behaviour can affect pupils' perception of themselves, leading to an impairment of self-esteem or in extreme cases 'a complete suppression of the spontaneous individual self' (Horney, 1939, p. 91).

Fortunately, as Justina's comment above demonstrates, pupils do not always accept negative definitions of themselves. She resists the idea that she is 'ignorant', preferring to think of herself as shy. Moreover, most pupils do experience situations, at home or with close trusted friends, in which they feel relatively confident. Pete described how not feeling shy was the time when he could 'just feel myself', and for Justina the opposite of being shy was 'ready ... to do anything', something which she experienced occasionally. In working to empower quiet pupils it is important for teachers to identify and develop situations in which all pupils can feel confident and able to 'do anything'.

Whilst quiet and withdrawn pupils agree that quiet or shy behaviour can be socially limiting they may have different, often contradictory, attitudes to talking in school. Anxiety about talking with, or in front of, others can prevent pupils from taking an active role in their learning. It can also make quiet pupils feel inadequate, especially in comparison with their more confident peers.

Mandy: I don't talk in class. I don't go out in front and talk in class 'cos too shy ... I don't know how others feel ... 'cos they might get used to it but I don't.

Because she is anxious about talking in front of large groups of relative strangers Mandy excludes herself from the public conversations of the classroom. By remaining quiet and allowing other, more vocal, members of the class to dominate discussions she denies herself valuable learning experiences in

21

which she would gain experience of talking and learn through talking. Some quiet pupils are all too aware that not talking in class prevents them from learning. For example, Justina talks with some emotion about the frustration she feels when her inability to talk freely in class prevents her from learning. She is also aware of an inherent contradiction in attitudes to classroom talk. She tries to comply with the teacher's request for 'quiet in class' but feels that prevents her from learning, 'but I'd still want to learn the questions and answers to ... to work and that so I know how to do it'. Incidentally, so far as the pupils are concerned, the notion of talk as a performance 'in front of others' is unique to their experience of school. In all other social situations their talk is more likely to be conversational with different expectations about how dialogue is initiated and sustained.

Anxiety about talking to relative strangers can contribute to poor self-esteem, especially when individuals compare themselves with more confident friends and relatives. Quiet individuals see an ability to converse easily as a skill to be envied and an inability to 'perform' in this way can make quiet pupils feel inadequate.

Charlene: Like my cousin, she talks a lot ... when she's at people's houses she doesn't know, she gets to know her very well ... after half an hour she starts talking ...

The pupils highlighted by this book try several strategies when attempting to overcome or cope with their shyness. These include pretending people are not there, trying to get into conversation by introducing a new subject, and trying to understand the other person's point of view.

Diana: Like if no one's talking to you right, you think to yourself how am I going to start a conversation but you think really that they're shy an' all, that's why they don't talk to you.

On occasions pupils simply walk away from social situations

22

in which they feel uncomfortable. However, whilst it may be an option to walk away from a socially embarrassing situation at home, this is rarely an option available to pupils in school. In school, teachers control classroom conversations and may require children to speak even if they do not wish to do so.

In working with quiet pupils, it is important to remember that whole-class discussions, in which the teacher dominates and controls the talk, can deprive quiet pupils of an opportunity to withdraw. Thus whilst a reluctance to speak can be a response to 'basic anxiety' (Horney, 1945) or the need for 'an inviolable privacy' (Guntrip, 1968), the teacher always has the power to ignore that need. In whole-class discussions, for example, the teacher is at liberty to call upon any pupil irrespective of their desire to talk. Thus, as was mentioned in the previous chapter, the teacher who values talk as an important medium for learning and wants to include all pupils is caught in something of a dilemma. They have to choose between allowing quiet pupils to 'opt out' of the activity, or subject them to the embarrassing ordeal of being made to talk. Neither option is satisfactory for either the teacher or the pupil. Knowing that they can be chosen to speak at any time adds to quiet pupils' anxiety. The fact that they are not in control and that they might feel 'shown up' in front of their peers can damage their already low self-esteem. As will be discussed in Part Three, small-group discussions where groups of children share responsibility for their feedback to the larger group are a powerful way of involving quiet pupils without them having to experience the embarrassment of speaking out on their own.

Anxiety about speaking in front of large numbers of relative strangers means that quiet pupils experience class discussions in a completely different way to their more confident peers. For confident pupils whole-class discussions are opportunities for them to voluntarily demonstrate their knowledge and power. By comparison, quiet pupils are anxious that they might be forced to speak against their will. The following examples will serve to illustrate the point.

Comparing quiet and more vocal pupils

As illustrated in Chapter One, Mandy is a quiet pupil who rarely volunteers to answer the teacher's questions, and never asks questions of her own during whole-class discussions. Consequently, such discussions give her little opportunity to 'name her world' (Freire, 1972). Invariably when she does participate it is at the insistence of her class teacher. On these occasions it is the teacher rather than Mandy who determines when she should speak. Mandy recalls how uncomfortable she feels when she is 'picked on' to answer a question in spite of not having her hand up: 'Horrible. I didn't like it. 'Cos I didn't know the answer ... I just sit there. Sometimes I gave him an answer ... but sometimes not'. In this situation she can appease the teacher by offering an answer, or she can attempt to satisfy her 'need to withdraw' by refusing to speak. Her obvious discomfort at being asked to speak suggests that neither response is easy or likely to enhance her self-esteem. This is such a negative experience that she can remember how often it has happened. In the following excerpt of the interview, Mandy talks about putting her hand up to answer a question.

JC: Does the teacher ever ask you to give an answer when you haven't got your hand up?

Mandy: Yeah. He asked me about five times

JC: Five times today?

Mandy: No. When I came in class ... last year ... he hasn't ... he hasn't told me ... this year ... just last year.

JC: So between September and Christmas you were asked five times?

Mandy: Yeah; about five times.

Unfortunately Mandy's account of classroom events suggests that the teacher does not choose her to answer as frequently as he did at the beginning of the academic year. It would appear that the teacher has 'learned' that Mandy is extremely anxious about being chosen to speak in front of the

24

class and is less likely to choose her when she doesn't have her hand up. Consequently, Mandy's anxiety about talking in class has led to a reduction in the number of times she is invited to participate in whole-class discussions. This confirms her negative impression of herself and denies her the opportunity to practise and improve her skills and confidence in this area.

By comparison, Mike, an extremely talkative boy, clearly enjoyed the opportunity to 'show off' during whole-class discussions. He invariably volunteered to answer the teacher's questions and was often chosen to speak. This may have been due, in part, to his tendency to call out his answer when other pupils were chosen to reply. In addition he was unlikely to be chosen when he did not have his hand up. Thus Mike had far more control over his participation in the discussion than Mandy was likely to experience. Moreover, Mike frequently asked the teacher questions during class discussions. On one notable occasion Mike asked a question which led to a conversation with the teacher that lasted several minutes while the rest of the class listened passively. Clearly Mike and Mandy can be seen to represent the opposite ends of a continuum. However, Mandy's experiences demonstrate how whole-class discussions deny quiet pupils the opportunity to take responsibility for their learning and 'name their world'.

Having established that exercising control over their speech could well be an important factor for quiet pupils, I have learnt to tolerate long silences from children, allowing them the opportunity to initiate conversation. Whilst this approach of 'waiting for the children to speak' is difficult if not impossible in whole-class discussions, it provided a breakthrough in my relationship with Vicky. Vicky is the most withdrawn pupil I have worked with. Her refusal to speak in school was so extreme that it bordered on elective mutism. Like the teachers and pupils who worked with Vicky on a daily basis, I began by compensating for her lack of speech with monologues of my own. However, observing how other people responded to Vicky's silence alerted me to the way in which this attempt at communication actually denied her the need to talk. On one occasion, for example, Vicky took her book to the teacher to be marked. The teacher, aware that Vicky was unlikely to talk, framed her response as a number of rhetorical questions and Vicky returned to her seat without speaking.

Clearly a different approach was needed. I discovered that Vicky was more likely to talk when I was prepared to be quiet and tolerate the inevitable long silences. Somehow the fact that I was not consciously trying to make her speak allowed her the freedom to speak for herself. This difference of approach could explain why Vicky talked freely at home. This experience certainly has serious implications for the education of all quiet pupils and especially those who might be termed elective mutes.

Relationships with peers

Primary schools are social institutions in which large numbers of pupils are expected to work and play together, often collaboratively on joint projects. In such an environment an ability to relate to one's peers and communicate freely with them is likely to be an important prerequisite for learning. Quiet pupils, perhaps even more than their confident peers, are aware that close friendships add to their feelings of security and enable them to settle down to face the challenge of learning in school.

For example, Diana regards being with close friends as an important prerequisite to learning, and being separated from her friends has an effect on her academic work as well as on her social life. She believes that her academic work suffered the year she was separated from her friend: 'I was bad last year 'cos I couldn't settle down properly'. That some pupils feel that they work better when they are with their friends has serious implications for classroom organization. I believe that peer relationships are important to all children and especially for those quiet pupils who experience anxiety in school. As a consequence, I advocate using friendship groups as the basis for small group activities.

In talking about her peers, Diana makes a sharp distinction between friends and acquaintances. Acquaintances may talk to you 'a lot' but, in some way which is difficult to explain, they cannot fulfil the same role as a friend. Diana had two close friends in primary school and, in contrast to many quiet pupils, she seems to have no difficulty in sustaining friendships. For example, she has been 'best friends' with Mandy since they started school together. Nevertheless, Diana recognizes that continual reassessment of relationships in school is time-consuming and can be disruptive both to participants and to observers. 'I had two friends sitting on my table and they was always arguing to one another and going "I'm not your friend now", right "I'm not your friend now" and they ... and they were always like putting me off my work.' Whilst disagreements are a feature of even the closest relationships, the level of pupil disharmony in school does suggest that an 'affective' or pastoral curriculum which examines the quality of relationships has value for pupils.

Having friends and being able to identify oneself as belonging to a particular group can add to an individual's sense of security. This can be particularly important in helping to deal with potential bullies. A lack of friends, inappropriate or ineffective social behaviour, and an unwillingness to talk to their teacher can make quiet pupils particularly vulnerable to bullying from peers. From her position of quiet observer Aberash made some shrewd comments about the way in which she and her classmates were bullied. She described the way in which a classmate was being subjected to 'psychological bullying' and the extent to which the victim's seeming nonchalance masked deep distress. Aberash concluded that whilst most people get teased at some time in their lives, those with a lot of friends were less vulnerable. 'Some people don't get teased at all 'cos like – em – it's like they've got friends – friend, and their friends got friends and everything – they like get hit and their friends come up, stop beating people up.' Aberash's observations led her to believe that friends are of more help than teachers in countering bullying. 'I see teacher dun't do anything but just telling them off.'

Few of the quiet pupils found it easy to make and keep close friends. They withdrew from contact with peers as much as possible and spent the greater part of their time alone. These 'social isolates' rejected attempts to include them in group activities and, perhaps as a consequence, were less likely to be chosen by peers. Other quiet pupils developed love/hate relationships which were in constant conflict, as if the pupils preferred antagonism to isolation. Whatever their response, pupils who experience difficulties in relationships with peers are unlikely to possess the skills for collaborative group-work activities.

The following account of Aberash's experiences illustrates the need for teachers to recognize the needs of quiet pupils and devise strategies which empower quiet pupils to work with their peers.

Aberash

When I first met her Aberash was a 'social isolate' or 'excluding' pupil. She spent much of her time in primary school alone. Even in busy, seemingly relaxed classrooms Aberash could be observed sitting alone in silence or standing passively near to, but not interacting with, other children. Moreover, she seemed to lack the skills to communicate with her peers and her infrequent attempts at making contact with them were often unsuccessful.

For example, at the start of the school day, when other pupils entered the classroom in groups amid a great deal of chatter, Aberash sidled in alone. She went straight to her place where she sat, unlike the majority of the class, on her own. As other pupils moved around the room and chattered with friends Aberash worked in total silence, seemingly engrossed in her work. No one approached her desk. After fifty minutes of this isolation Aberash got up and stood behind Mandy's chair. Eventually, seemingly irritated by Aberash's silent presence, Mandy asked what she wanted. At this Aberash shrugged her shoulders, tapped Mandy on the shoulder and moved back to her seat where she remained for the rest of the lesson. To an observer it seemed as if Aberash wanted to make some kind of contact with Mandy but lacked either the confidence or the social skills to be able to do so. On reflection, it is interesting that Mandy, another quiet pupil, challenged Aberash with 'What do you want?' rather than initiating a conversation which would encourage her to stay and talk.

Her mother associated Aberash's reluctance to socialize with the fact that she came from a different infant school from her classmates. 'She found it difficult to fit into, you know like the knowledge they all had of each other before, you know with knowing so and so since we had been in nursery so we know this person. This person fits in as a talker, this person fits in as a quiet one, this person fits in as a victim, this one the bully.' However, withdrawn behaviour (which might have been regarded as understandable hesitancy on the part of a new pupil with no knowledge of her peers), persisted to some degree throughout her attendance at primary school. When invited to comment on Aberash's imminent transfer to secondary school, one teacher said that her behaviour was so aloof it 'was almost as if she had never really arrived'.

Aberash's physical isolation from other pupils in the school seemed to be reinforced by her body language and demeanour. Even when invited to join in a group activity Aberash would often maintain a physical distance from the other members of the group. Moreover, her facial expression rarely changed from one which could be interpreted as blank sufferance. Her stepfather suggested that body language has to be interpreted in terms of cultural norms. 'Culturally if you go back in the Caribbean, black children do not look in the teacher's face, it's a sign of insolence. In this country "Look at me when I'm talking to you" – see?' This observation develops the notion of possible contradictions and conflict between the cultures represented by home and school. However, Aberash's stepfather reflects a cultural stereotype in saying that, coming from an 'oral tradition', West Indians 'gesticulate more'. This is a view which is clearly not borne out by observations of Aberash's behaviour in school.

29

However, her stepfather was close to the truth in suggesting that Aberash's teacher never saw her laugh; her expression in the classroom was, typically, serious and 'shut in'. In so far as her unwillingness or inability to express a range of emotions is a response to 'basic anxiety', this suggests a deep unhappiness or fear. A rigid adherence to this one mode of behaviour may have served as a barrier to communication between Aberash and others in the class. It certainly suggests a repression of a happy carefree aspect of her nature, which might well be described as a 'denial of self'.

Not surprisingly, when Aberash was asked to work with a partner she resisted, saying that she preferred to work alone. Even in the relative security of a small group withdrawn from the classroom, she took several weeks to accept the idea that she could work with others. During the research she became increasingly more relaxed as she got used to working with specific trusted individuals. Moreover, as relationships developed she was observed laughing and joking with her new-found friends. On these occasions it was striking how relaxed and expressive her body movements could be.

This increased confidence in relationships was also evident in Aberash's social life outside school. Her mother noted a change in Aberash's behaviour towards children of her own age. Aberash was 'making more contact with the kids she's at school with, she's actually wanting to make more contact with them, like meeting them before school to go to school together'. For her mother this represented a change in behaviour as previously Aberash 'had a separate existence from school than at home'.

Difficulty with relationships with teachers

Irrespective of their relationship with peers, the quiet pupil's inability or unwillingness to talk freely in school is likely to be related to difficulties in their relationships with teachers. For example, just as the term 'excluding' adequately describes Aberash's behaviour towards peers, it is also an appropriate description of her relationship with teachers. Her mother made a connection between Aberash's facial expression and her relationship or, more accurately, lack of relationship with her teacher. 'He finds it hard to find out what mood she's in because she always seems to be on that deadpan face straight mood he doesn't know how to gauge her mood.'

Aberash's mother describes an inability or reluctance to communicate with her teacher which concurs with observations of Aberash working in the classroom.

> She doesn't let him in, she's very ... she doesn't communicate with the teacher on a one-to-one basis; as much as possible she doesn't talk to the teacher that she's with at the moment and he finds that difficult because he thinks that he would be able to help more as a teacher if she would talk to him but she doesn't like the teacher she doesn't talk to him unless he talks to her, she's not going to compete with other kids and actually ask questions and she doesn't initiate any contact with him unless she really has to do.

This passage is quoted at length because it touches on many of the basic themes of this book.

First, implicit in the comment about the teacher's inability to help Aberash because she will not talk is the notion that education takes place through dialogue. Speech is a powerful way in which pupils make knowledge their own and demonstrate what they have learnt. Yet Aberash avoids all but essential dialogue with her teacher, and even then the conversation is perfunctory and she 'doesn't let him in'. Little wonder that teachers spend less time over the stilted, one-sided, conversations which are the best that they achieve with quiet pupils like Aberash, and concentrate on developing links with their more demonstrative pupils. Sadly, this represents something of a self-fulfilling prophecy, as those who have most difficulty in communicating with their teachers have less opportunity to improve through practice.

Second, it demonstrates the need for positive relationships between pupils and teachers. When, as in Aberash's case, there is no rapport between pupil and teacher the relationship could be viewed as a source of suspicion or even fear, rather than as a secure base from which to 'venture out' into the unknown. Neither Aberash nor her mother says why she dislikes this otherwise popular teacher. However, given the lack of relationship between them, it was particularly unfortunate that they were forced to work together for two years.

Finally, Aberash's mother suggests that one of the reasons why Aberash does not approach the teacher for help is the need to compete with other pupils in the class. Certainly this book provides evidence of the difficulty which quiet pupils face in getting or holding their teacher's attention. For obvious reasons potentially disruptive pupils invariably get the attention they demand either in whole-class discussions or on a one-to-one basis. Yet observations suggest that when quiet pupils make similar moves, such as putting their hand up or going to the teacher's desk, they receive less of the teacher's time and are often sent away or simply ignored. Thus even when quiet pupils pluck up the courage to talk with their teacher they are less likely to be rewarded for their action than are their more boisterous peers. The way in which the needs of quiet pupils can be overlooked is best illustrated with reference to other quiet pupils.

The anxiety which quiet pupils experience when talking with people they do not know well can be acute. Moreover, when the teacher gives the impression that talking in class is inappropriate, or even naughty, quiet pupils are likely to 'comply' with the request for silence. Rasheeda's lack of communication with her teacher implies a parallel lack of relationship. She does not talk to her teacher much ''Cos he has to work, some work to do and I have some work to do and if I say like speak to him a lot, he says just carry on with your work'. She seems unaware that both she and the teacher should be engaged in the same task, her education. The way in which quiet pupils exclude themselves from learning relationships is also demonstrated by Diana's comment about what she sees as the teacher's role. 'When I'm stuck he has to help me … work and everything but most of the time he's …

he's like talking hisself like doing things on the board and things so you can't really talk to him when he's trying to learn children.' In this account she effectively precludes herself from any participation in whole-class discussions for fear of disturbing the teacher. Moreover, she does not include herself in the group of children being taught. Her passivity is confirmed.

The need to compete with other pupils may contribute to quiet behaviour during whole-class discussions. However, Aberash's initial reticence during small group activities and her seeming reluctance to talk freely with me during one-to-one interviews suggests that there are other factors involved. Her stepfather describes her as 'somebody that's probably got a lot of things inside which she's trying terribly hard to get out'. Similarly her mother said 'You have to work hard to get at who she is'. Whatever the cause of her quiet behaviour, the discussion of the relationship between language and learning in Chapter One confirms that there are powerful educational reasons why it is vital to allow Aberash, and pupils like her, to 'get at who they are'. In addition the move towards self-realization is a basic human need.

During the research, Aberash's strained relationship with her teachers became evident and was particularly acute during the first in a series of one-to-one interviews. Here conversation was one-sided and Aberash seemed extremely reserved. Her responses were characteristically short and often difficult to hear. An example of the difficulty in initiating a flowing conversation is illustrated by the passage in which Aberash was asked about her trip to Jamaica. An open-ended question such as 'What is Jamaica like?' led to a long pause and eventually to the response: 'I don't know'. However, Aberash gradually warmed to the subject and described some of the bird-life she had seen. 'We saw some big birds ... like storks ... and we saw ... we saw two humming birds. They like, they hover over like sticks with wings coming out ... they stay in one place then they start moving again.' This short description is represented in the transcript by five lines of speech interjected with encouraging noises from me and lengthy silences.

Similarly, in subsequent interviews Aberash gave interesting accounts of her involvement in activities both in and out of school. This illustrates an 'eloquence of intention' as well as her interest in the activities themselves. However, as such accounts were delivered in a quiet monotone, 'active listening' required close attention and a tolerance of long pauses. Whilst such support is relatively easy to provide during a one-to-one interview, the pressures of classroom life may make it a relatively rare event in a child's daily experience of school.

In the context of one-to-one interviews Aberash was prepared to share something of her inner feelings. In the first interview it was significant that Aberash described herself as someone who 'didn't talk a lot' and went on to say that whilst being shy was 'normal' it could be a disadvantage in social situations, 'like when we went to this woman's house, didn't know her very well ... she asking if I wanted this and I went ... just shook my shoulders'. Aberash is clearly frustrated at being silenced by fear in social situations, and one can imagine the way in which parents and other adults respond negatively to what they perceive to be rude behaviour. The possible importance of such a revelation was self-evident during the interview. However, the relevance of other comments only became evident during the careful transcription of the interview and in conjunction with information gathered from other sources.

One such example occurred at the start of the first interview. Aberash had been asked to describe her 'personal time-line' which she had completed previously and had in front of her as an *aide-mémoire*. She talked about learning to swim and temporarily losing her confidence. Perhaps because of her quiet and expressionless style of speech, it was only on transcribing the interview that it became clear that Aberash linked this loss of confidence with her mother having to go to work. 'Then she had to ... sometimes she had to go to work then I was a ... then when I had to go to the swimming baths again I was afraid to go in the water.' The possible effect of Aberash's separation from her mother will be discussed in Part

Two. The important issue here is that if it is difficult to hear and respond appropriately to Aberash in a one-to-one situation, how much more difficult it must be for teachers to 'hear her' in a busy classroom. Indeed, learning to recognize and overcome such failure to communicate is one of the main themes of this book.

* * *

In this chapter I have shown that pupils who are quiet and withdrawn in school often feel anxious about talking in front of others, especially large groups of relative strangers. The anxiety that quiet pupils experience when asked to talk in front of others clearly disadvantages them during whole-class discussions. Quiet pupils are often frustrated that their behaviour prevents them from making the most of the educational opportunities presented to them. Related to their anxieties about talk, quiet pupils also have difficulties in forming and sustaining relationships with peers. They also have poor relationships with teachers in school. Having established the characteristics of quiet withdrawn pupils, the account next focuses on different types of quiet withdrawn behaviour.

3 Types of withdrawal

As was discussed in the previous chapter, an individual's anxiety about talking and poor relationships with teachers and peers may contribute to the quiet behaviour we witness in schools. Later in the book I will also explore how relationships with parents (Part Two) and inappropriate teaching styles (Part Three) may also contribute to quiet behaviour in school. However, whilst the cause of quiet behaviour was particular to individual children, the behaviour of most quiet children in the classroom followed a similar, and therefore predictable, pattern. During my research I identified four types of withdrawal exhibited by quiet pupils. I describe these as 'being invisible', 'refusing to participate', 'hesitation' and 'an inappropriate focus'.

The following accounts of these four types of withdrawal should help teachers to identify quiet withdrawn pupils and provide a basis for reducing the incidence of non-participation in school. However, whilst habitually quiet behaviour is detrimental to learning and should be discouraged, for some pupils at least, occasional withdrawal may be the only way they can cope with overwhelming anxiety. I conclude this chapter with three incidents in which pupils exhibited a 'need to withdraw'. Such incidents are of particular importance to teachers as they have clear implications for classroom practice.

Four types of withdrawal

In some situations pupils would have no direct contact with the teacher during a lesson. Often there was evidence to suggest that where the pupils sat or how they behaved made them 'invisible' and minimized their contact with the teacher. Alternatively, pupils would be invited to participate but would 'refuse' to join in. Sometimes the refusal would be direct and possibly supported by a seemingly valid reason. On other occasions the pupils would not acknowledge the request; they would remain quiet and avoid making eye contact with the teacher. Whilst these two forms of non-participation were relatively easy to detect the other two presented more of a problem and required closer observation. In both of these situations the pupils appeared to be busy but closer analysis revealed that the pupils were not actively engaged in the task set by the teacher.

In the third form of non-participation pupils exhibited 'hesitation' and would remain on the periphery of an activity. They appeared busy but never really became engaged in the task. Sometimes they seemed to be afraid of participating. The final, and to my mind the most disturbing, form of non-participation was that in which pupils had 'an inappropriate focus'. In these instances pupils would be actively involved in an irrelevant task. This concerned me, because in the majority of instances the teacher was either unaware of what the pupil was doing or, worse, condoned the behaviour.

During the observations I came to associate different forms of non-participation with specific groups of children. For example the most withdrawn pupils would have little contact with their teacher and were unlikely to initiate a conversation. When they were asked a direct question these pupils would refuse to answer or else they would provide the minimum of information. Vicky seemed especially able to become 'invisible' in the classroom. By contrast, anxious pupils like Roxana were more likely to hesitate on the periphery of activities. On occasions these pupils would attempt to join in with their peers but would then, for whatever reason, need to withdraw.

Whilst there were general trends in the ways in which groups of pupils behaved, individuals might, at different times and in different situations, exhibit a range of behaviour. For example, during a period of two days that I spent shadowing

Justina in her secondary school she exhibited all four forms of non-participation discussed here. In order to provide continuity the following discussion is based on the observations of Justina's non-participation. However, the analysis of these observations is supported with reference to the behaviour of other pupils.

The following discussion has two aims: first, to describe the non-participatory behaviour; second, to suggest what might have been done in that specific situation to empower the pupils concerned to participate. The question of how far the pupils' observable behaviour was deliberate, unconscious, learned or innate is unanswerable and to some degree irrelevant. Of particular significance to classroom teachers is how pupils can be made aware of their behaviour and be encouraged to try alternative approaches. The ultimate aim would be for pupils to have a wide repertoire of 'ways of being' from which they could choose a form of behaviour which they judged to be the most appropriate in specific situations.

Being invisible
In 1988 James Pye used the phrase 'invisible children' to describe pupils frequently overlooked by their teachers. I regarded pupils as being 'invisible' when they had no direct contact with their teacher. Given that my sole reason for being present during lessons was to shadow specific pupils, I was surprised that I should observe any instances in which these pupils were being ignored by their teacher. I had thought that my very presence would be sufficient to put these pupils 'in the spotlight' during the lessons I observed. However, during the course of the study I witnessed a number of lessons in which there was no direct communication between teachers and specific pupils.

Isolated incidents of 'being invisible' may not have a significant effect on a child's learning. In fact in some situations individuals may benefit from the experience of working independently and without close supervision. However, as Harry Guntrip (1968) emphasized, 'becoming a person' requires that two seemingly contradictory aspects of personality are recognized and 'held in balance'. 'It is hard for individuals in our culture to realize that true independence is rooted in and only grows out of primary dependence' (p. 268).

A strong sense of separate identity develops through feelings of connectedness with significant others. Thus when pupils are allowed to 'become invisible' in the classroom they are being deprived of feelings of connectedness with teachers and other pupils. Moreover, the importance of getting practical support from their teachers was expressed by the pupils themselves. In an interview, Justina linked what she saw as her teacher's refusal to help with the fact that she found mathematics difficult. In the same interview she also talked passionately about her needs for her teacher's support. 'When I went to, for him to help he told me to go back and sit down ... and that's why I got them all wrong ... and that it weren't fair.' Despite this belief in the value of teacher support, I observed a number of instances in which Justina was unwilling, or unable, to talk to the teacher about her work. The following is an account of one such occasion.

The incident occurred during a craft lesson in which groups of pupils worked independently on predetermined craft projects. Throughout the lesson, and even when the teacher visited the table where she was working, there was no obvious communication between Justina and the teacher. When discussing the project on which Justina was working the teacher spoke to, or was answered by, the other two girls on the table. During this time Justina stood slightly to one side, head bowed, totally still and totally silent. Although the teacher did not address her directly there were several instances in which Justina could have joined the conversation had she been willing and able. Observing this incident it seemed that both the teacher's behaviour and Justina's reticence contributed to the lack of communication between them. Had the teacher asked Justina a direct question it might have been easier for her to join in. As it was, Justina's seemingly more confident peers dominated the discussion about their work. As the conversation progressed it struck me that these two girls were claiming ownership of their project in a way which Justina never did. However, there was a sense in which Justina's exclusion from the discussion was self-inflicted. At no point did she attempt to join in the discussion. Moreover, her physical isolation from the group and her refusal to make eye contact seemed to discourage engagement. Thus Justina's 'invisibility' in the classroom came about partly by the teacher's actions and partly because of her own inability or unwillingness to participate. Observing other quiet pupils in similar situations, I speculated that their difficulties were related to limited social and conversational skills and poor self-esteem. In addition, my observations confirmed James Pye's (1989) assertion that where pupils sit and how they behave in the classroom contributes to a tendency to be ignored by the teacher. A discussion of the ways in which pupils use and dominate space in the classroom (or fail to do so) concludes this account of 'being invisible'.

In many of the lessons I observed, the pupils remained seated throughout the lesson. However, when movement was allowed or considered appropriate it was interesting to note who dominated the physical space of the classroom. During the course of my research I noticed that quiet withdrawn pupils tend to occupy a smaller physical space than their more dominant peers. For example, in the primary school the class could be divided into three broad groups according to the degree to which they moved around the room and dominated the space. Although the teacher regularly told the class to work quietly at their desks, pupils varied considerably in the degree to which they carried out this instruction or the degree to which they were allowed to disregard it. One end of a continuum was typified by quiet pupils who hardly ever got out of their place. When they did, it was for a specific reason, for example to collect equipment or at the express request of the teacher. These pupils were unlikely to approach the teacher or initiate contact with him. As has been suggested throughout, habitual reluctance to talk with the teacher must inhibit learning.

By comparison, there was a small group of about half a dozen boys who constantly moved about the room, chatting to their friends or disturbing those who were trying to work. These boys blatantly disregarded the teacher's instructions to sit quietly, and seemed to get up whenever they chose. They were rarely chastised by the teacher, who occasionally tried, usually with some success, to coax them back to the task in hand. Watching this class it was clear that the predominantly female quiet pupils were restricted to their own desks whilst the more outgoing boys literally had the run of the room, which they seemed to dominate. When the activities extended beyond the classroom, for example when there was a computer set up outside in the corridor, the boys would wander in and out of the room at will. Comments made by staff during an assembly suggest that these boys also dominated the playground.

Between these two extremes was a third group of pupils, predominantly quiet boys. They appeared to want to be recognized as 'one of the boys' and claim the rights and respect attributed to that group. However, whilst individual pupils aspired to join in with the dominant boys, other people's perceptions of them prevented them from doing so. An example will serve to illustrate the point.

The incident involves Duncan during his last year in primary school. During a lesson in which the class were asked to work quietly at their desks, Duncan observed a group of pupils, especially Daniel and Dale, ignoring the teacher's instructions and wandering round the room chatting to friends on the pretext of borrowing crayons. After a while Duncan got out of his seat and walked over to a friend seemingly with the express wish to make arrangements for some activity taking place after school that night. However, whilst the teacher seemed prepared to allow Daniel and Dale some leeway, the same was not true when Duncan tried to assert himself. In a tone which he did not use with the other boys the teacher barked out an instruction to 'Go to your place' and Duncan, easily chastised, scuttled back to his place which he did not leave again that lesson.

Believing that where pupils sat in the room was likely to affect the amount of contact they had with the teacher, I was interested to notice how many times the 'quieter' girls sat round the edge of the room whilst the boys 'dominated' the centre space. However, the reasons why pupils sat where they did were difficult to determine. It would be tempting, for example, to suggest that the boys chose to sit in the middle of the room in order to get the maximum attention from the teacher. However, I noticed on more than one occasion how girls entering the classroom first would 'claim' their space near the walls of the room before the boys arrived. It was not so much that the quiet pupils did not claim their space in the classroom but rather that the space they claimed was likely to be small and at the margins of the room. Clearly the use and domination of classroom space is a complex issue, and I remain fascinated by the implicit social rules which determine peer hierarchies. In the context of this book the important issue appears to be the need for teachers to be aware of, and try to involve, those pupils who are potentially 'invisible children'.

Refusal to participate

I use the term 'refusal to participate' to describe occasions on which pupils were invited to take part in a discussion or activity, but refused. In some cases the pupil would offer a reason for their refusal, and in others they would simply hang their head and refuse to speak.

An incident in which Justina refused to participate happened at the start of an English lesson. The pupils were being reminded that their homework from the previous lesson was to prepare a short talk on a subject of their choice. When Justina was asked to give her talk she said that she could not because she had been off school during the previous lesson and was not aware that homework had been set. The teacher accepted this excuse and Justina sat through the rest of the lesson in total silence, not even joining in with the discussion of other pupils' talks. Given that Justina was quiet and shy, she may have been relieved that the teacher did not press her to 'perform' on this particular occasion. However, my observations of Justina, over time and in a number of situations, suggest that this refusal to participate was all too common. Earlier the same day Justina was not able to take part in a computer activity because she had not finished the previous task.

Participation in classroom activities could be organized in such a way as to help develop an individual's self-confidence and feelings of being valued and of belonging. If talking in front of the class is considered too difficult for pupils like Justina, there are several simple alternatives. First, pupils could work in small groups, presenting their talks to a few trusted individuals. Secondly, pupils could work together on joint presentations thus relieving some of the pressure of working alone. Thirdly, the pupils could be given or, better still, draw up for themselves, a few simple rules or criteria by which their talk should be assessed. In this way the teacher could explicitly acknowledge the difficulty of the task whilst at the same time breaking it down into manageable activities.

My experience of working with quiet pupils in primary and secondary schools is sufficient to convince me that relatively quiet pupils can be encouraged to meet the challenge of oral work so long as they understand exactly what is being expected of them. Another important requirement is that they feel confident that their participation will be respected. Experience also suggests that these strategies are beneficial for all pupils, not just those who tend to be quiet or withdrawn. In the English lesson mentioned above, the majority of the pupils delivered their talks but none of them did so particularly well. All the pupils seemed unduly nervous and ill-prepared.

Hesitation

In some lessons Justina did attempt to join in with class activities but her participation was minimal or 'hesitant'. In my observations there are many examples of this kind of behaviour in which she seemed to be on the fringe of an activity. In craft, for example, Justina spent significantly more time watching her partners working than she did actively engaged in the task. Similarly, during a practical lesson Justina walked round the science lab, touching some of the equipment with the tips of her fingers but rarely carrying out the intended experiment. On both occasions she seemed reluctant to 'get her hands dirty' by handling the equipment.

The consequence of this behaviour in science was that whilst several pupils completed all the tasks relatively quickly, Justina, who visited all the experiments, completed less than half and could only give a garbled account of what she had done. Thus it would seem that on this occasion at least her learning had been detrimentally affected by her inability or unwillingness to become involved in the lesson. Whilst other pupils could clearly cope with the lesson, I feel that Justina would have benefited from a more structured approach. Perhaps working with a partner around a predetermined circuit of activities would have helped to provide her with a clear focus.

On some occasions I could not understand why pupils were hesitant about joining in with an activity. However, during one maths lesson in which pupils were being assessed on their ability to build three-dimensional shapes, the cause of Justina's hesitation was clear. She was afraid. Watching her check and double-check her measurements, often rubbing out what appeared to be perfectly acceptable lines, her anxiety was evident. This anxiety may not have been caused solely by the presence of a particularly strict, one might say aggressive, teacher. However, his brisk comment that 'This should have been finished by now' and his concluding remark ('If you have done three you have done well, if you have done two you have been trying, if you have done one I don't want to see you next week') must have contributed to her concern.

Whilst one might argue that such a 'bullying' approach has little place in any classroom, such remarks may be particularly damaging to the (already low) self-esteem of some quiet pupils.

Once again, Justina's progress was severely hampered by her hesitation during the lesson. Whilst the majority of the pupils completed three or more models, Justina just managed to finish her first despite having 'worked' solidly throughout the lesson.

Inappropriate focus

By comparison, in other lessons Justina appeared to be working 'on task', fully participating in the activities of the classroom. However, closer inspection of what she was actually doing during those lessons suggested that she had an inappropriate focus. On occasions this inappropriate focus was being encouraged, or at least condoned, by her teacher's comments.

The most obvious example of this occurred during a French lesson. Throughout the lesson, including during oral work, Justina was hard at work, writing in her exercise book. She had even taken the initiative of devising her own dictionary of 'new words' in a separate book. Judging from the comments in her exercise book the teacher was highly delighted with her progress. On page after page, she was complimented for the neat presentation of her written work. Encouraged by this praise, she had armed herself with a number of coloured pens, rubbers and paper whitener, in a quest to maintain these standards of neatness.

Yet despite her diligence I felt that Justina had missed the central point of the lesson, since she did not speak a single word of French. Her one interaction with the teacher was conducted in English and focused on a point of detail about the setting out of her work. He seemed oblivious to her lack of participation in the oral part of the lesson. When, out of sheer frustration, I asked Justina to read what she had just written she said: 'I don't speak French because it confuses me.' Justina's compliance with her teacher's expectations for her written work was matched by an equally stubborn refusal to share the language with anyone.

What, I wondered, did Justina expect to learn during the

French lesson? For me, Justina's stubborn refusal to learn to speak a second language was the most obvious example of an educational experience failing to make an impression on an individual's view of the world. By allowing, or encouraging, Justina to have such an inappropriate focus to her work, the French teacher was actively denying her the right to 'allow the knowledge presented to her to make any deep impact upon her view of reality' (Barnes, 1979, p. 17).

In other, less extreme, examples Justina's attention seemed to be focused on irrelevant, or at least less significant, aspects of the lesson. During a computer lesson, for example, Justina and her partner spent several minutes choosing the background colour for their work. Over the same time-scale many of their peers had become engrossed in the problem-solving activity. Similarly, Vicky spent the whole of a science lesson fetching materials for other pupils. In both of these lessons the pupils needed to be reminded of the main focus or aim of the lesson.

To summarize, my observations of quiet pupils at work in their classrooms suggest that non-participation can be described as fitting into one of four categories: being invisible, refusal to participate, hesitation and inappropriate focus. An awareness of the way in which quiet withdrawn behaviour can be detrimental to learning enables teachers to consider ways of empowering their pupils.

However, in encouraging quiet pupils to take a more active role in their education it is important to consider the needs of the individual pupils. During my observations it became clear that, for some pupils at least, withdrawal was a defence from overwhelming anxiety. A discussion of the emotional and behavioural needs of pupils who habitually exhibit quiet withdrawn behaviour leads to the notion that extreme or habitual withdrawal should be considered as a form of special educational need. The consequence of creating a 'new category of need' is discussed in Chapter Four of this book. I would argue that, in so far as quiet pupils experience emotional and behavioural difficulties, teachers have to take account of their special educational needs. One of the most important ways of doing this is to allow pupils the emotional space to withdraw when necessary.

The following section describes incidents in which pupils need to withdraw as a result of experiencing and trying to cope with their acute anxiety.

A need to withdraw

During my observations three pupils demonstrated their need for what I have called 'emotional space' in the classroom. In all three cases the pupils' need for withdrawal is related to their being afraid. The incidents in which the pupils demonstrate their anxiety are very different, as are the pupils' individual responses to it. Yet in their own way, each of these pupils showed a need for someone to recognize and contain their fear. Perhaps it is significant that, in two incidents, those involving Roxana and Susie, the possible cause of their distress was clear, whilst in Duncan's case I never found out what had triggered his anxiety.

As the following accounts will demonstrate, observing these pupils at a time of acute anxiety made me realize just how debilitating their fear could be. It also convinced me of the need for us to treat pupils' anxiety as real, and respond sympathetically even if the underlying cause is not known. However, coping with pupils at times of acute distress is a useful reminder of the great, sometimes conflicting, pressures which are inherent in teaching. In some cases these pressures prevent us from responding to individuals' anxieties in the way they might prefer. There seems little opportunity in the average school day for teachers and pupils to 'take time out' in order to discuss issues which are of particular and often immediate importance to individual pupils.

Roxana: A pupil afraid
As is discussed in an illustrative case study (Chapter Seven), anxiety related to performing in front of a group of pupils

47

from another class transformed what had been a confident and able musician into a quivering wallflower. In Roxana's case her need to withdraw from the activities of the classroom was as sudden as it was dramatic. The teacher was so busy orchestrating the activities of the rest of the class that he had no time to spend with Roxana, beyond expressing his frustration that she should choose that particular moment to 'act up'. Having the time to observe Roxana closely, I was convinced that this was neither an act nor a deliberate attempt to sabotage the lesson. I feel that it is not too dramatic to say that Roxana was totally overcome by anxiety at the mere thought of the forthcoming performance. This was all the more surprising because, throughout the lesson, Roxana had demonstrated her significant talents on a number of musical instruments.

Duncan: Moving in uncontained space

Like Roxana, Duncan also underwent something of a character transformation. He sat quietly through a maths lesson working conscientiously and with some success on the tasks set by the teacher. Yet when he arrived at the science lesson which immediately followed it he was giddy, excited and hyperactive. As I noted at the time, the best description of his behaviour during the science lesson was of a pupil moving in an 'uncontained space'. He appeared to have little or no control over his speech (loud and rambling) or his actions. His movements were so uncontrolled as to present a real danger in the science lab, surrounded as he was by Bunsen burners and other scientific equipment. As with Roxana's anxiety, the teacher was clearly aware of the problem but the pressures of simultaneously co-ordinating a number of practical experiments did not allow him the time to talk with Duncan.

The fundamental difference between the incidents involving Roxana and Duncan is that in the latter case I can offer no explanation for the dramatic change in behaviour. I had walked with Duncan from one lesson to the other and, as far as I am aware, nothing was said or done to make him anxious. As the science teacher was one of the teachers whom Duncan had nominated for me to interview, I had assumed that this was a teacher whom Duncan liked and therefore neither the teacher nor the lesson was likely to make him unduly anxious. I was left wondering if Duncan had simply become tired by his unusual exertions in the maths lesson and needed time and space to rest.

Susie: A fundamental misunderstanding

Whilst the previous two examples demonstrate dramatic changes of behaviour which were noticed by the teacher concerned, Susie's distress was far more low-key. Indeed, so far as I could tell, it went completely unnoticed by the class teacher. Throughout the lesson Susie looked unusually miserable. More or less ignoring what was going on around her, all her attention seemed to be focused on a letter which she turned over and over in her hand. Wanting to know how things would develop, I waited until the end of the lesson before asking what the problem was. It turned out that having fallen and bumped her head during break time, Susie had been sent to the member of staff responsible for first aid for a 'bump form' to take home that night. Unfortunately the person concerned had, as was the school's custom, addressed the envelope to the pupil's mother.

Susie knew that this was wrong; her mother had left home some years previously and Susie now lived with her father and stepmother. Yet to ask for the letter to be changed meant publicly acknowledging the situation. This was especially difficult for Susie as she had not become reconciled to the loss of her mother. In one-to-one interviews Susie spoke with some emotion of the time when her mother would return to the area, shower her with presents and suggest that they live together as the ultimate happy family. Clearly, it was easy to imagine how, with this background, the letter would assume a major significance to Susie. The immediate issue was easily resolved when a new envelope was found and properly addressed. Dealing with the deeper anxiety connected with the loss of her mother and the acceptance of a stepfamily would take much longer. My only regret was that my role as researcher prevented me from acting much sooner. If I had done so Susie would have been saved some anxiety and she would have had the opportunity to concentrate her energies on the lesson in hand.

Underlying all these incidents is the observation that pupils who 'come undone' as the result of acute anxiety are not in a good position to cope with the challenge which school has to offer. It is because anxiety inhibits learning that teachers need to help pupils to recognize and work through the causes of their distress. Incidents like those cited above demonstrate how offering pupils appropriate emotional support becomes an education issue. It also suggests that some pupils with deep or prolonged anxiety may benefit from some form of counselling or therapy.

*　　*　　*

I began this book with the premise that habitually quiet behaviour is detrimental to learning. In this chapter I provided an account of different types of withdrawn behaviour in the hope that it will help teachers to identify and reduce instances of non-participation in schools. However, whilst advocating greater pupil involvement, I am also aware that for some pupils occasional withdrawal may be the only way they can cope with overwhelming anxiety. As ever, the challenge for teachers is to decide when it is appropriate to encourage individual pupils to participate and when it is best to leave well alone. Understanding the specific needs of individual quiet pupils is an important first step in offering appropriate support. In the next chapter I review some of the research on special needs and debate the degree to which quiet pupils should be regarded as having special educational needs.

4 Special educational needs

Habitually quiet withdrawn behaviour is detrimental to learning, yet pupils who exhibit such behaviour are often invisible in the classroom, ignored by their teachers and peers. In order to highlight the plight of these pupils I would argue that we should regard pupils who habitually exhibit quiet non-participatory behaviour as having special educational needs and that recognizing those needs is an important first step in empowering pupils to play a more active role in their education. My reasons for linking habitually quiet behaviour and special educational needs are twofold. First, quiet non-participatory behaviour is, of itself, detrimental to learning (see Chapter One). Second, quiet behaviour is often associated with, or caused by, emotional difficulties such as anxiety, poor self-esteem and difficulties in forming relationships with others (see Chapter Two).

However, defining special educational needs is difficult and fraught with contradictions. The identification of need is likely to lead to the provision of appropriate support but may also result in discriminatory labelling. Through a review of selected literature I examine the current special needs debate and highlight a number of key issues which are relevant to the education of habitually quiet pupils. This chapter includes discussions of:

- the legal definition of special educational needs
- the limitations of the traditional definition of emotional and behavioural difficulties and the need to consider the plight of quiet pupils
- the implications of different definitions of need for perceptions of need and potential solutions to difficulties

- the advantages of terms like 'needs', 'rights' and 'opportunities' in the education of quiet withdrawn pupils

I conclude the chapter with a discussion of the need to integrate definitions of need and considerations of pupils' rights and opportunities.

The legal definition of special educational needs

In 1978 the Warnock Report (DES, 1978) recommended that the existing categorization of disability was educationally inappropriate and should be abolished. The Committee proposed that such categories be replaced with the generic term 'learning difficulties' which could be further described as 'mild', 'moderate', 'severe' or 'specific'. In the Warnock Report, and the 1981 and 1993 Education Acts, the terms 'special educational need' and 'learning difficulty' are used interchangeably.

The change in terminology, from categories of handicap to more generic and flexible concepts, represented a major development in special education. It was an attempt to remove the formal distinction between handicapped and non-handicapped students and to encourage the integration of pupils into mainstream education (Fish, 1989; Roaf and Bines, 1989). Moreover, it reflected a shift in emphasis from medical or psychological criteria of assessment and placement towards an educational, interactive and relative approach which would take into account all the factors which could have a bearing on educational progress. Thus special educational needs were considered to be individual and they were defined for the first time in terms of the curriculum, the means of access to it and the social and emotional environment in which it was taught.

The Warnock Report (para 3.19) defined special educational needs as being likely to take the form of need in one or more of the following areas:

i)   the provision of special means of access to the curriculum through special equipment, facilities or resources, modification of the physical environment or specialized teaching techniques;

ii) the provision of a special or modified curriculum;

iii) particular attention to the social structure and emotional climate in which education takes place.

These three broad-based areas could be used to cover most, if not all, aspects of education. However, in work with quiet withdrawn pupils with behavioural and/or emotional difficulties, the emphasis on the 'social structure and emotional climate' is of supreme importance. For these pupils their special needs are fundamentally associated with the quality of the relationships which they are helped to develop in school. In this context, issues of specific teaching techniques and an appropriate curriculum follow naturally from good relationships and a supportive environment.

In many respects, then, the recommendations of this book correspond to the three ways of meeting special educational needs as identified by the Warnock Report. However, in considering ways in which counselling and/or therapy can help some individuals to address the root causes of their quiet behaviour, I depart from the Warnock recommendations.

The 1981 and 1993 Education Acts

Following the Warnock Report, the 1981 and 1993 Education Acts also define special educational needs in relative terms. Special needs are seen as learning difficulties of all kinds rather than as individual defects. Moreover, special educational needs are seen as arising from physical, sensory or intellectual disabilities and not as identical to them (Fish, 1989). However, one of the major effects of the definition of need offered by the Education Acts is that need has become inextricably linked to the provision of extra resources: 'For the purposes of this Act a child has "special educational needs" if he has a learning difficulty which calls for special educational provision to be made for him.' In terms of this definition, it is debatable whether or not the majority of quiet withdrawn pupils can be considered to have special educational needs. I would argue that the majority of resources needed to empower quiet withdrawn pupils are well within the scope of ordinary class teachers in mainstream school. The fact that the social and emotional climate of many classrooms is not conducive to active pupil participation does not mean that the necessary changes in relationships or teaching styles should be regarded as either 'extra' or 'special'. As will be demonstrated in Part Three, the 'resources' needed to meet the needs of the majority of quiet pupils are good quality pupil–teacher relationships and supportive learning environments with appropriate use of small group activities.

It is only in cases where pupils need support, in order to deal with major crises or unresolved issues, that the additional resources of trained counsellors or therapists are needed. However, given the number of children traumatized by family breakdown, bereavement and abuse, I would suggest that there is a need for all teachers to receive some training in counselling skills. At the very least teachers need to be able to identify those pupils who need, or would benefit from, additional specialist support. In addition there is a growing body of evidence to support the view that such specialist support is especially effective if provided by appropriately trained members of staff within the school (Cooper, 1993). Again, this suggests that resources to meet the needs of quiet pupils should be readily available to all, and not provided as additional or special resources for a minority of pupils defined as having special educational needs.

However, the definition of 'learning difficulties' contained in both the 1981 and 1993 Acts does not preclude pupils who habitually exhibit quiet withdrawn behaviour. According to the Acts, a child is considered to have learning difficulties if:

a) he has a significantly greater difficulty in learning than the majority of children of his age; or
b) he has a disability which either prevents or hinders him from making use of educational facilities of a kind generally provided for children of his age in schools, within the area of the local education authority concerned, for children of his age; or
c) he is under the age of five years and is, or would be if special

education provision were not made for him, likely to fall within para (a) or (b) when over that age.

(Education Act, 1993, section 156)

So far as quiet withdrawn pupils are concerned it is clear that they are not able to make 'use of educational facilities of a kind generally provided'. Consequently, quiet pupils must be regarded as having special educational needs. Moreover, much of the quiet withdrawn behaviour witnessed in school has its origins in emotional and behavioural difficulties which do comprise a recognized category of special educational needs. However, I understand a reluctance to describe the origins of their quiet behaviour as a 'disability'. The term disability suggests both within-child factors and a medical model of handicap which denies the social factors of need as defined by Oliver (1988).

The following section examines ways in which the definition of emotional and behavioural difficulties needs to be modified to encompass pupils who habitually exhibit quiet non-participatory behaviour.

A revised definition of emotional and behavioural difficulties?

In the context of this book the connection between habitually quiet behaviour and special educational needs is clear. However, in many respects making this connection is paramount to creating a new definition of emotional and behavioural difficulties. Whilst emotional and/or behavioural difficulty is the second largest category of special educational need identified in school (Beveridge, 1993) it is not normally used to define habitually quiet behaviour. The reasons for this are discussed below and are related to what is considered to be socially acceptable behaviour.

The nature and extent of emotional and behavioural problems are wide-ranging and, apart from the most severe cases, difficult to define. Teacher judgements are based on their professional experience and are likely to incorporate comparisons with the general standard of conduct in the class. Inevitably though, they may also be influenced by personal values and expectations about what is considered to be appropriate social and emotional behaviour. Typically, boys are more likely than girls to be identified as having emotional and behavioural difficulties, as are pupils from particular minority ethnic backgrounds (Tomlinson, 1982).

It has been suggested (for example, ILEA, 1985) that teachers are less alert to signs of emotional difficulty that create problems for the individual pupil than to the more overt behaviour that presents them with problems of class control. Others (for example, Croll and Moses, 1985) argued that teachers differentiate between problems of discipline and other forms of educational and behavioural difficulty. This view is supported by Beveridge (1993, p. 49) who suggests that 'on the whole, it would seem that pupils are identified by their teachers when their behaviour is judged to interfere with their own learning or that of other pupils, or to disrupt their relationships with peers and staff'. However, evidence suggests that quiet withdrawn pupils are often overlooked in busy classrooms. Moreover, the fact that few writers include habitually quiet behaviour in their definition of disaffection implies that the term 'emotional and behavioural difficulty' is more likely to be used to define loud, disruptive and potentially aggressive pupils.

One possible exception is the definition of disaffection offered by Paul Cooper (1993). In *Effective Schools for Disaffected Pupils* he begins by including withdrawn behaviour within his definition of disaffection. Moreover, in talking about the difficulties which teachers experience in trying to motivate pupils he implies that withdrawal and disruption are opposite ends of a continuum of anti-social behaviour. He describes how the teacher's optimistic and positive intentions 'are met with apathy, are ignored or, worse (?) openly resisted and disrupted' (p. 2). He implies, therefore, that apathy and disruption may be equally serious. However, with this one exception the book defines disaffection exclusively in terms of disruptive, potentially aggressive behaviour. Cooper is concerned with the 'common ground' covered by such terms as 'disaffection', 'problem behaviour', 'emotional and/or behavioural difficulties' and 'deviance'. He also examines the way in which these terms are used to 'describe behaviour that is perceived to be in some sense deviant and problematic to the smooth running of the organisation in which they are applied' (p. 3). The emphasis on loud potentially disruptive behaviour implies that the concept of special educational need is a form of social control and is used primarily for those pupils who cannot be easily controlled in mainstream classes or who hinder the smooth running of the school.

The link between special educational needs and social control was emphasized by Ford and his colleagues who asked: 'To what extent, therefore, is the establishment of special education provision an expression of the wish to control a deviant section of the school population?' (Ford *et al.*, 1982, p. 27). Certainly, it is easy to see how social control could be a powerful motivation behind special needs provision for loud aggressive pupils. However, work which aims to empower quiet pupils and enable them to experience alternative forms of behaviour is more difficult to define in these terms. Whilst quiet behaviour is detrimental to both individual learning and emotional development, seemingly compliant pupils do not offer a threat to school discipline and consequently the needs of such pupils are unlikely to be either identified or met. Nevertheless, many of the recommendations made by Cooper (1993) are also appropriate for quiet withdrawn pupils.

By including quiet withdrawn pupils in the definition of special needs, this book accepts a wider definition of need, one such as that proposed by Mel Ainscow and Jim Muncey (1989, p. x). In *Meeting Individual Needs* they endeavour to carry the definition offered by the Warnock Report (DES, 1978) to its logical conclusion by arguing that all pupils have special educational needs and 'not just those who at some time for some reason depart too far from some mythical expected standards and rates of progress'.

This is a significant development from the narrow 'deficit model' definition which preceded the Warnock Report. However, as the following discussion will illustrate, there are problems and limitations to the notion of individual need and what Roaf and Bines (1989) have called 'the cult of individualization'. The tensions inherent in the 'special versus individual' needs debate emerge in the following discussion of different approaches to need as proposed by Mike Oliver (1988).

Different approaches to special educational need

In a chapter entitled 'The Social and Political Context of Education Policy' Mike Oliver (1988, p. 13) argues that there are three different approaches to the definition of disability and special need. He implied that the approach to, and consequently the definition of, disability has changed over time: 'Initially, disability was perceived as an individual problem; it then came to be seen as a social construction and, finally, it is beginning to be perceived as a social creation.' Thus Oliver implies a clearly defined and developmental shift in the approach to, and definition of, disability. An examination of what is meant by each of the three terms 'individual problem', 'social construction' and 'social creation' highlights the relative merits of each approach and introduces the key issues which pervade the special educational needs debate as it relates to quiet withdrawn pupils in mainstream school. This discussion also suggests, contrary to Oliver's definition, that the three ways of looking at the issue of need are interrelated and that a combination of approaches is in fact the most helpful in defining and meeting individual needs.

Needs are an individual problem
Oliver (1988) suggests that this definition underlies most approaches in the field of professional practice adopted by

teachers, social workers, doctors, occupational therapists and psychologists. Stated simply, this position maintains that it is the individual with the disability who has the problem, and intervention aims to provide the individual with the appropriate skills to cope. In terms of the quiet withdrawn pupils highlighted in this book, this type of definition would suggest that the problem lies solely in the individual's inability to form relationships with others. This is a medical model which implies that the individual has a clearly defined problem which can be reduced or cured by appropriate treatment.

One major criticism of this approach is that it emphasizes what are seen as deficiencies within the individual, which can lead to categorization and labelling of pupils. The relative merits and demerits of categories and labels remain a dilemma for all teachers working in the field of special needs. Some writers (for example, Ainscow and Tweddle, 1988, p. 69) believe that all labels and categories are essentially discriminatory and should be abolished.

> Instead we should find ways of acknowledging the individuality of each pupil, that all children experience learning difficulties and that all can experience success. The aim must be to organise schools in ways that help teachers to respond to, and indeed celebrate the personal qualities and interests of each member of their class. The achievement of this would be to the benefit of all pupils.

Thus an approach which emphasizes pupils' strengths rather than their weaknesses is of benefit to all pupils. Indeed, Part Three of this book demonstrates how appropriate teaching strategies can raise pupil self-esteem and empower quiet pupils to take a more active role in their own education. Paradoxically, this can only be achieved after the detrimental effects of habitually quiet behaviour are realized and the possible root causes of quiet behaviour are identified. This suggests the value of identifying the specific needs of a group, whilst not underestimating the potential of individual pupils.

Roaf and Bines (1989) acknowledge the value of an individual approach but go on to argue that in view of the 'pre-judice and discrimination in our society' (1989, p. 94) it is not sufficient merely to abandon the labels. Instead, they argue that for teachers to be effective advocates for young people they have to be 'able to recognise characteristics in common, not to encourage stereotyped reactions, but as a way of recog-nizing that there are important group differences between people which are a valued part of their individuality' (p. 95). The need to be able to identify common characteristics without resorting to crude stereotypical reactions is a theme which runs throughout this book. An example will serve to illustrate the point. For some pupils, their quiet withdrawn behaviour could be related to early or prolonged separation from primary attachment figures. However, as the case studies in Part Two show, it would be inappropriate to assume that all pupils from lone-parent families are equally affected by the absence of the other parent. Moreover, deviant attachment can occur in two-parent families. As with all work with children, the balance between common characteristics and individual need is a delicate one which can only be achieved in schools when teachers begin to know, and relate to, their pupils as individuals.

Roaf and Bines (1989) valued the individual approach to need but they also realized the limitations of such an approach. They argued that to treat an individual, under-achieving because of class or race issues at school, simply at an individual level is neither adequate nor effective. The argu-ment here is that since so many needs arise from expressions of social, ethnic or other group prejudice and discrimination, failure to alert the school and society to the needs of these groups is also a large part of the failure to meet individual needs. Roaf and Bines conclude with the statement that 'while the larger structural issues remain unaddressed so will indi-vidual approaches remain cosmetic' (p. 95). This suggests that work which aims to empower quiet withdrawn pupils has to consider both the possible root causes of an individual's behaviour and the social environment in which the behaviour occurs. The social component of need is highlighted in subsequent discussion of different approaches to need.

Needs are socially constructed

Oliver (1988) suggested that many academics and writers who have taken an interest in special needs see needs as socially constructed. This definition has also been relied upon heavily by policy-makers who seek to solve problems redefining disability. According to this argument the problem lies in the fact that some human beings define others as disabled, and therefore treat them differently. This type of definition maintains that if you change the way in which people think about disability you eliminate the problem of disabled people. Thus a logical consequence of redefining special educational need to include pupils who exhibit quiet withdrawn behaviour is likely to alter the way in which such pupils are regarded by their teachers. A positive outcome of a change in the definition of need could be that the specific needs of an overlooked section of the school population are identified and met. Indeed, as this book illustrates, many quiet pupils would welcome such changes. An analysis of pupils' perceptions of themselves reveals that not only do they define themselves as quiet or shy but that they perceive this to be detrimental to both their social life and academic learning. Moreover, the pupils were also aware of the difficulties which they experience in asking their teachers for help.

However, whilst it is important for the teaching profession to acknowledge the needs of quiet withdrawn pupils there is a danger that this could lead to negative or stigmatized labelling of individual children. The negative effects of using categories and labels to describe children is long established. In *How to Reach the Hard to Teach* (1984, p. 33) Paul Widlake went so far as to argue that 'the process by which we label pupils may turn out to be more influential in causing learning difficulties than any other activities teachers engage in'. Thus a definition which regards need as socially constructed implies a desire to disregard disability and to treat everyone as if they were

61

normal. However, as Roaf and Bines (1989) point out, the issue of relevant and irrelevant difference is a highly complex area which cannot be avoided by anyone concerned with needs and rights, and one which has proved to be a major stumbling block. They argued that simplistic remarks such as 'We all have special needs', 'All children are special' or 'I don't see them as black or white/girls or boys, they're all just children to me', originate in a genuine confusion about when a difference is relevant and when it is not. The important but difficult task for the teacher, as for the manager of scarce resources, is to be able to distinguish between the two in a way which is just and fair. 'To ignore differences altogether, or to pay too much attention to irrelevant differences, are both equally unjust' (p. 93). As quiet withdrawn behaviour is detrimental to learning, such behaviour has to be regarded as a 'relevant difference' and should be identified as such by teachers. However, recognizing need without negative labelling requires delicate handling.

Needs are socially created

The third approach suggested by Oliver (1988) is that needs are socially created. This position is often articulated by disabled people and has involved intense disputes with able-bodied professionals and academics about what the problem actually is. This position argues that society disables people with impairments by the way it responds to those impairments. For example, any limitations in the means of access to buildings stem from decisions to design them in particular ways and not from the inability of some people to walk. The solution to this particular problem is to create a barrier-free environment, not to attempt to provide disabled people with the skills necessary to cope with steps. There is a growing trend toward the disabled community defining disability and need (Barton, 1988). Moreover, disabled people are increasingly determined to control their own lives and are vociferously expressing their views both as private persons and through their own associations (Wade and Moore, 1993a).

Not surprisingly, this has led to tensions as criticisms are expressed not only over the role of professionals in the lives of disabled people, but also over the way in which able-bodied people are constant sources of oppression and dehumanization (Sutherland, 1981).

In the case of quiet withdrawn pupils, the social creation of need would maintain that these pupils are silenced not by their innate inability or unwillingness to communicate but by an environment which does not allow them sufficient space and encouragement to talk. 'Thus, inappropriate teaching materials and techniques may be seen as having generated or at least exacerbated the range of learning difficulties experienced by pupils' (Roaf and Bines, 1989, p. 6).

As Part Three of this book demonstrates, appropriate teaching styles and an emphasis on the quality of relationships in school are frequently sufficient to empower pupils to take a more active role in their own education. However, I realise how difficult it is for teachers like myself to accept that schools may cause or exacerbate pupil difficulties. Accounts of children's disaffection in schools which focus attention exclusively on family background factors are not uncommon (Cooper, 1993). Moreover, 'those who over emphasise family and individual pathology explanations can be blind to the influence which they and their institutions can have on these problems' (p. 14). In particular, teachers can be unaware of the extent to which the very possession of such views can interact with the problem situation and so exacerbate, and in some cases create, further difficulties.

In addition, as Cooper (1993, p. 17) illustrates, the most vulnerable (those who experience humiliation, fear or anxiety) 'are the very people in the school system who are likely to be given least opportunity to voice their concerns'. It is difficult for quiet pupils to find a voice in the classroom. It is also difficult for members of that community to accept both the change in behaviour and the possible criticisms which may accompany it. For example, a teacher is likely to feel threatened by pupils' remarks about unfair treatment when their request for help is denied. Similarly, black pupils could seriously upset the status quo of the classroom if they expressed concerns about the lack of multicultural or anti-racist material readily available in school.

Combining different approaches to need

Whilst Oliver suggests three distinctly different approaches to the subject of need, I would argue that these are not mutually exclusive and can exist simultaneously. For example in *Educational Opportunities for All?* (1985, p. 4) the Inner London Education Authority offers a description of disability which almost captures all three approaches: the individual, the social constructionist and the social creationist view of special educational needs.

> Disabilities and difficulties become more or less handicapping depending on the expectations of others and on social contexts. Handicaps arise from the mismatch between the intellectual, physical, emotional and social behaviour and aspirations of the individual and the expectations, appropriate or otherwise, of the community and society at large. Individuals with disabilities or significant difficulties may be handicapped by their own attitude to them and by the attitude of others. Of equal significance, the degree to which the individual is handicapped is determined by the educational, social, physical and emotional situations which he or she encounters. Handicapping effects will vary from situation to situation and may change over time.

This passage is quoted at length because it illustrates something of the myriad of complex factors which combine in the definition of disability or need. In the context of work with quiet withdrawn pupils a similar point can be made with reference to the different factors which underlie an individual pupil's quiet withdrawn behaviour. For example, as illustrated in Roxana's case study (Chapter Seven), quiet behaviour can be seen in terms of an individual need and an inability or unwillingness to talk freely in class. This could be related to Roxana's 'anxious attachment' to her mother during early childhood. Conversely Roxana's quiet behaviour can be discussed in terms of the social context of the classroom. Her quietness may be a response to teacher-directed talk which precludes active pupil participation. Similarly, she might be silenced by a fear of being bullied by her peers. On the other hand, if Roxana has been criticized for talking in class she is likely to believe that talking is naughty or even anti-social. Whatever the underlying cause of Roxana's quiet withdrawn behaviour, it has to be discussed in terms of her individual need as expressed in specific social contexts and in the light of prevailing views about the nature of talk and learning. Thus Oliver's three ways of defining need are inextricably linked.

Need as an inappropriate concept

Despite the changes in definition of special educational need, it remains a very difficult and complex concept in practice. 'It has the appearance of simplicity and familiarity, yet its use in so many contexts, the fact that it appears to have both normative and non-normative meaning and that it is essentially concerned with values and priorities, should alert us to its complexity' (Roaf and Bines, 1989, p. 9). This is especially true at the present time when we are already a long way from the days when it was only handicapped children who were perceived as having needs.

In a chapter entitled 'Needs, Rights and Opportunities in Special Education' Roaf and Bines (1989) suggest four reasons why 'need' is a problematic term.

The first criticism is that the term 'need' is ill-defined and consequently too broad. It is often used in relation to the development and learning of all children. Given their individuality and idiosyncrasy, defining what constitutes a special educational need in any particular case can be difficult. The arguments for and against the inclusion of quiet withdrawn pupils in the category of *special* educational need offer a clear illustration of some of these difficulties.

The implications for using a broad and ill-defined term like 'need' are especially serious when such a term is used as the basis for special resource allocation. Another related difficulty with the term 'need' is that whilst 'special educational needs' is now the generic term, the number of specific descriptive categories has not been reduced. Indeed the Warnock Report and 1981 Act, while attempting to remove the difference between handicapped and non-handicapped pupils, did not take special education out of the realm of handicap. Instead, more students have been brought within its brief under the much broader and ill-defined category of 'learning difficulty', and further divisions have emerged, particularly between students who have statements of special educational need and those who do not. Indeed, the broadening of the definition of need is illustrated by the fact that, in the context of this book, the generic term 'special educational need' is being extended to include habitually quiet pupils.

The second criticism offered by Roaf and Bines is that the relativism of needs as currently understood can lead to haphazard and unequal provision. 'Special educational need' is a legal and administrative term as well as an educational and descriptive one, thus taking on different meanings according to the context in which it is used. Such relativism is also a feature of the legislative definitions within the 1981 and 1993 Education Acts, where need is defined in terms of the level of difficulty experienced by children and the kind of educational provision available. Being considered to have special educational need may, therefore, largely depend on which school a child attends and in which locality, leading to considerable variation in assessment, placement and subsequent educational treatment. This relativism and unequal provision may be partially responsible for the fact that quiet withdrawn pupils are not recognized as having special educational needs. As was suggested in the introduction, loud potentially aggressive pupils are more likely to come to the attention of harassed teachers in busy classrooms than their quiet peers. Seemingly compliant behaviour can easily be confused with a commitment to learning.

The third criticism is also related to this relativism and is that needs are a matter of professional and value judgements. Roaf and Bines argue that the moral and political basis of such judgements are usually neglected because we still focus on the *receiver* – the individual or group with needs. Yet hidden within these conceptions of needs are social interests (for example, to make the disabled productive or to control troublesome children) together with a range of assumptions about what is *normal* (Tomlinson, 1982). By focusing on needs, and particularly by taking assumptions about the nature of those needs for granted, we do not ask who has the power to define the needs of others. We do not enquire why it is the professionals who mostly define needs, as opposed to parents or the students themselves. Nor do we fully explore the normative nature of our assumptions – for example, that they are grounded in conceptions of 'normal' cognitive development or behaviour, whether such assumptions are informally operated by teachers in the classroom or more formally operated by normative testing. The focus is on what seem to be the genuine needs of the individual who lacks something and who has a need. However, that needs may be assessed by valuing certain aspects of development and attainment more than others is not considered .

The final criticism, and one with particular significance to work with quiet withdrawn pupils, is that the term 'needs' has now become a euphemism for labelling individuals as 'special'. This is partly due to its hidden implications and partly to limited change in traditional approaches and practice. The idea of having a difficulty suggests something can be done about it. Thus the concept of 'needs' remains deficit-based, despite attempts to relate it to context, with an inbuilt tendency to slip back towards individuals and their problems. However, it could be argued that despite its individualistic approach to difficulties and handicaps, the term 'special educational need' also clouds issues of values, power and function (Tomlinson, 1982). In short, despite intentions to limit stigma and labelling, it 'has become a new euphemism for failure' (Roaf and Bines, 1989, p. 7).

The concept of 'need' is inadequate on its own as a means of achieving the goals of education for those identified as having special needs. I believe that the discourse of equal opportunities and rights, with its emphasis on entitlement, provides a more effective base for policy and practice.

Needs, rights and opportunities

Replacing the concept of needs with that of rights and entitlement has a number of advantages. First, thinking in terms of rights and opportunities links the special needs debate with other equal opportunity initiatives, for example, the Sex Discrimination Act (1975), the Race Relations Act (1976) and the development of the concept of equal opportunities in education from the mid-1970s onwards (ILEA, 1985; Potts, 1986). Thus special education becomes part of a larger struggle for equality, and racial or gender dimensions of being 'special' can also be raised. A lot of work has already been done on equality of opportunity in other areas – for example, class, gender, race – on which the special needs debate could draw (Adams, 1988; Byrne, 1985; ILEA, 1985). Inequality is now understood as both structural, institutional and interpersonal and strategies to deal with each of these levels have been established (Lynch, 1986; Straker-Welds, 1984). Moreover, it is understood how discrimination, and therefore lack of opportunity, may be subtly or indeed explicitly reflected in aspects of schooling such as the curriculum and teaching materials. Teachers could apply this understanding in relation to special educational needs. Equal opportunity is also an effective touchstone for evaluating provision.

The connection between different aspects of discrimination is of particular relevance to quiet withdrawn pupils. Evidence suggests that several of the pupils highlighted in this book were discriminated against in a number of ways. The majority of the pupils were working-class girls. Moreover, the experiences of the four black pupils suggests a clear link between race and other forms of discrimination.

As Roaf and Bines (1989, p. 12) summarize, it would seem to be

> beneficial to operate the more radical notion of opportunity,
> arguing for positive discrimination in terms of staffing or
> resources in order to ensure that children and young people
> experiencing impairment or other difficulties do get full benefit
> from ordinary education. It would also seem worthwhile to make
> the connections between disadvantage arising out of class, race
> or gender and disadvantage arising out of special needs as
> traditionally perceived.

This implies a redefinition of the concept of need and an accompanying reappraisal of resource allocation. Nevertheless, equality of opportunity still seems to imply being dependent on others and on making something of yourself, which not all young people can do.

The second benefit of linking needs with issues of rights and opportunities is that it should 'free us from individualized, deficit-based approaches to special needs and enable us to consider ways in which the entitlement and rights of children designated as having special needs can be ensured and extended' (p. 1). Considering issues of rights and opportunities implies a move away from a deficit-based approach, which in turn re-emphasizes the social construction and creation of disability and need. More fundamentally, to regard children with special educational needs as children whose rights are being infringed in some way would 'substantially alter the status not only of children themselves, but also of special needs teachers and others who work on their behalf in their negotiations with the educational hierarchy' (p. 13).

For Bandman (1973), being perceived as having rights 'enables us to stand with dignity, if necessary to demand what is our due without having to grovel, plead or beg'. Having need is too often associated with a lack of dignity and respect. As Freeman (1987, p. 300) argued:

> Children have not been accorded either dignity or respect. They
> have been reified, denied the status of participants in the social

system, labelled as a problem population, reduced to being seen as property. Too often justice for the young has been trumped by considerations of utility or, worse, of convenience.

The emergence of children's rights as an important social and political issue is thus to be welcomed. However, in the 'rights' approach there are difficult issues to be faced by educators. First, there has been much confusion generally between liberal (access) and radical (outcomes) versions of the equality debate (Evetts, 1973). Secondly, for the individual, the issue of rights implies identification with a group of similarly disadvantaged people. Thus talk of 'rights' can presume a level of categorization which may well seem contradictory to special needs teachers who have been encouraged to abandon categories. Thirdly, it can be difficult to achieve equality of opportunity without encountering contradictions such as the difficulty of balancing normalization with the need for positive discrimination and provision. Such difficulties may be even more pertinent to debates about special educational needs because physical and other impairments may not just mean overcoming structural disadvantage and discrimination but also providing compensatory measures.

An integrated approach

Rather than abandoning 'needs', it may be more appropriate to ensure that they are put back in their place: that is, 'as a means of identifying, from a set of wide-ranging and often interlocking circumstances or characteristics, those which apply in a particular case, be it an individual or a group' (Roaf and Bines, 1989, p. 14).

The problem with 'needs', as currently understood, is that it is a term which often serves to mask category and disadvantage without actually specifying or overcoming these in any way. Indeed, an unintended effect of the Warnock Report and subsequent Education Acts is that 'needs' has become a category as in 'special needs children', gathering together widely different groups who are then assumed to be defective in some way.

Perhaps it should be recognized that, even with a radical stand-point, students are not helped by teachers unable to look at specific needs and provide appropriately for them. The question is not whether quiet withdrawn children have needs; all children do. The real issue is to identify the nature of those needs and how they are constructed, perceived and maintained.

Thus, 'needs statements' in themselves should not be regarded as a sufficient basis for developing policy and practice, because of the tendency to reinforce individualized, deficit-based approaches. Instead, needs should be tied to entitlement of rights and opportunity, in order to emphasize a systems approach and to strengthen and assert the interests and equity of those considered to have such needs. This would also remove some of the burden of guilt and stigma which is still associated with having special educational needs. 'To be entitled to something is very different and more positive than to need it, since it gives both validity and value to the claim' (Roaf and Bines, 1989, p. 15).

This emphasis on entitlement underlines one of the major aims of this book, which is to empower quiet withdrawn pupils to take a more active role in their own education. Part One has focused on the pupils themselves. Part Two examines the role of parents and especially the possible connections between inappropriate parent–child relationships and the quiet withdrawn behaviour witnessed in schools.

Part Two
The Parents

5 Quiet behaviour and the parent–child relationship

In Chapter Two I argued that quiet withdrawn behaviour may be related, at least in part, to the quality of relationships which exist between parents and children. From extensive interviews with quiet children and their parents it becomes obvious that patterns of relationship established during early childhood can influence an individual's self-image and affect their ability and willingness to enter into relationships with others.

Through a re-examination of John Bowlby's attachment theory I discuss the need for a balance of separation and connectedness in 'good enough' relationships. Next I discuss the parental role and introduce the notion that both mothers and fathers can be prime attachment figures for their children. Having established what constitutes 'good enough' parenting I then focus on two potentially problematic aspects of the parent–child relationships, namely 'anxious attachments' and 'separation'. I conclude the chapter with a summary of the implications for teachers and relationships for learning in schools.

Attachment theory re-examined

Attachment theory was first postulated by John Bowlby in 1969. He defined attachment theory as 'a way of conceptualising the propensity of human beings to make strong affectional bonds to particular others' (1977, p. 201). He described 'attachment behaviour' as that which results in a person 'attaining or retaining proximity to some other differentiated and preferred individual', the 'attachment figure', who is usually 'conceived as stronger and/or wiser', and thus better able to cope with the world (1989b, p. 129). Thus Bowlby's view of the parent–child relationship is one in which the infant has an innate propensity to seek stimulation and promote attachment to significant others, who will provide protection and support.

Besides the need for close contact, the attachment theory also supposes a second innate tendency: the urge to explore the outside world. Bowlby hypothesized that the infant's urge to explore and play, which takes them away from their attachment figure, counteracts a need for safety through proximity. The knowledge that an attachment figure is available and responsive provides a strong and pervasive feeling of security. The child can tolerate separation from their attachment figure when their memory of them is secure. The term 'secure base' was first used by Bowlby's colleague Mary Ainsworth (1967), to describe an infant's use of an attachment figure as a base from which to explore. Bowlby emphasized the important role for parents in providing the child 'with a secure base [and encouraging] him to explore from it' (1977, p. 206). Central to Bowlby's account of attachment theory is the notion that the disruption of an attachment bond can be distressing. Whilst the threat of loss is associated with anxiety, the actual loss of an attachment figure is associated with sorrow; both are likely to arouse anger. Bowlby acknowledged that attachment bonds could be a source of both security and potential distress. Thus the ambiguity which exists in all parent–child relationships is implied but not explicitly stated.

The 'good enough' relationship

According to attachment theory, children who have 'good enough' relationships with their parents experience an age-appropriate level of separation and attachment with their attachment figures. In such a relationship the parent achieves the difficult balance of meeting the individual's needs without forcing themselves on the child in ways and at times which the child does not want or need. Through a balance of these elements of security and freedom in a relationship an individual can develop a sense of both 'self' and 'other'. In good enough relationships the parent sets limits on the child's behaviour, thus protecting the child from the disintegration that occurs when the absolute self has its way. Thus the child's ability to recognize the parent as a person in their own right, with their own needs, is a significant stage in the child's development of self-identity as a separate person.

The need for a balance of separation and connectedness in relationships may be widely acknowledged. However, it has to be recognized that in a patriarchal society these two qualities are not ascribed equal value. In a patriarchal society independence and separateness are associated with masculinity and are valued over the 'female traits' of dependence and connectedness. Perhaps because girls tend to be mothered by someone of the same gender, they develop more fluid or permeable ego boundaries than boys, and a sense of self that is continuous with others. In turn, this sense of self-in-relationship and need for connection underlies the desire to mother. As subsequent case studies will illustrate, girls tend to be defined, by themselves as well as by others, primarily as future 'wives and mothers, *thus in particularistic relation to someone else*' [my emphasis] (Chodorow, 1978, p. 178). In addition girls often adopt mothering roles in their relationships with siblings and significant others; for example, Diana accepts her father's description of her as a 'little mother to her sister'. Thus, regardless of whether or not they become mothers, motherhood is central to the ways in which women are defined. By comparison men are defined primarily in universalistic occupational terms. Indeed, in a patriarchal society, it is considered weak and effeminate for men to describe themselves in terms of their relationships with others.

Nevertheless, given that self-realization grows out of relationship with others, the connection between independence and dependence is clear. Moreover, a critical review of post-feminist literature on parenting leads to the assertion that to talk in terms of 'male' and 'female' traits is an inappropriate social construct. The traditional male and female dichotomy denies that these traits are simply aspects of an individual's personality which ought to be recognized and held in balance.

Muriel Barrett and Jane Trevitt begin their book *Attachment Behaviour and the Schoolchild* (1991, p. 8) with a description of children who feel secure enough about their attachments within the family to be able to accept the transition to school without undue anxiety. 'They have learned to tolerate separation from those who are important to them (attachment figures), secure in the knowledge that reunion will follow.' It is important to note that what makes these children 'secure' is the ability to tolerate separation from attachment figures. This reinforces the view that, far from being harmful, pre-school experience of separation and reunion are essential for a smooth transition from home to school. Secure pupils appear confident and can relate positively to their teachers and peers. They expect others to respond positively towards them, they are able to wait for attention, and are not overwhelmed by apparent rejection. Such children are self-reliant and can be observed finding solutions to problems independently or in co-operation with their peers. They show a responsive interest and a lively curiosity in a school environment that is initially unfamiliar to them.

Whilst all the pupils highlighted by this book habitually demonstrate quiet non-participatory behaviour, an analysis of the quality of parent–child relationships suggests that some of these pupils have secure attachments with a parent or significant other. This suggests that secure attachments with parents are a necessary but not sole condition for active involvement in the social and academic life of the classroom.

Other factors, for example, the quality of relationships (teacher–pupil and amongst peers) in school, teacher expectations, teaching style, and potential conflict between the values of home and school, may also contribute to the quiet non-participatory behaviour witnessed in school. (For a discussion of strategies which have proved useful in overcoming these factors and empowering quiet pupils to play a more active role in their education, see Part Three).

Attachment figures

In describing a child's first relationship, Bowlby placed great emphasis on the role of the mother as prime carer. His belief in the existence of monotrophy ('the bias of a child to attach himself especially to one figure', 1989b, p. 389) was supported in his own work by the fact that in the studies he quoted, only those children who were living with their natural mothers were selected for observation. Yet even among these children several patterns of attachment emerged. Several children were said to be attached to both mother and father, whilst one child 'whose mother was in full time work, chose grandmother who looked after him most of the day' (p. 306). Thus whilst Bowlby admits the possibility that the prime attachment figure could be someone other than the natural mother, such cases appear to be 'deviant' rather than healthy alternatives. The importance of the 'specific mother figure' is implied throughout his work.

The notion of the 'specific mother figure' as a child's primary attachment figure was challenged by research into the relationship between strong attachment and general sociability (Main and Weston, 1981). In observations of some sixty infants it was found that children may have secure relationships with either parent, both parents, or neither parent. Moreover, in their approach to new people and new tasks the children reacted in different ways along a continuum. Children with a secure relationship with both parents were most confident and most competent; children who had a secure relationship with neither were least so; and those with a secure relationship with one parent but not the other came in between. Evidence that general sociability can be linked to the quality of parent–child relationships has clear implications for teachers and especially in work with habitually quiet non-participatory children in school.

Anxious attachments

The notion of anxious attachments has been with us for some time. In *The Making and Breaking of Affectional Bonds* (1977) Bowlby described four deviant patterns of attachment behaviour which may manifest themselves at any stage of life from childhood through to adulthood. The deviant patterns are 'anxious attachment', 'compulsive self-reliance', 'compulsive caregiving', and 'detachment'. Whilst his distinction between the different types of attachment has been influential in therapeutic work, I suggest that it is less useful to teachers working in mainstream classrooms. More appropriate for the needs of teachers and researchers are the three types of anxious attachment as described by Muriel Barrett and Jane Trevitt (1991). The following discussion is based on these three types of anxious attachment: 'overprotection', 'confusion' and 'rejection'. This distinction can help to explain the behaviour which pupils exhibit in school. Moreover, it gives some insights into the teacher–pupil relationships which exist, or need to be formed, in order to provide children with the 'secure base' which is a prerequisite for learning.

Overprotective attachment
Barrett and Trevitt (1991) describe overprotection as a relationship in which the parent is unable to allow the infant to explore independently, with the result that the child has few opportunities to learn to survive separately. The resulting relationship is sometimes referred to as symbiotic or 'smothering mothering'. A child with an overprotective parent is rarely allowed to experience frustration as all their needs are met immediately. Consequently they have no chance to develop problem-solving strategies nor can they discover that frustration and anger can be survived. This can result in omnipotent behaviour with the child never discovering that their wishes are not demands. Alternatively, children can grow up fearful and unable to cope; for example when they are in school, they are expected to be independent and self-reliant. Without any

experience of individualization the child cannot develop a realistic sense of self.

Duncan's behaviour serves as an excellent example of the way in which fearful behaviour in school is linked to overprotective parenting. Duncan was a diminutive boy living with both his natural parents and two much older boys from his mother's previous marriage. His mother admitted that his older brothers would be overprotective towards Duncan. 'They used to pass him things without him having to speak for them or anything, and we used to say you must ask him for what he wants otherwise he won't be able to talk.' Yet there appeared to be a contradiction between what she knew to be in Duncan's best interest and the way she behaved towards him.

In school Duncan was an unhappy child, frequently reduced to tears over seemingly minor incidents. Anxious about his inability to settle after his transfer to middle school, his mother became a 'teacher's helper', regularly visiting Duncan's classroom to assist with art or project work. During her visits Duncan would work alone, seemingly happy to ignore her presence. However, at the end of her visit he became very distressed at her leaving. Both Duncan and his mother seemed oblivious to the fact that such displays of behaviour might be considered inappropriate for a child of 8 or that they made him vulnerable to taunts and teasing from his peers.

In his mother's absence Duncan would seek out and 'cling' to members of staff, trying to hold their attention with constant, often irrelevant and unstructured monologue. However, he habitually avoided contact with peers and showed extreme reluctance to answer questions in class. Duncan's peer-avoiding behaviour continued when he transferred to secondary school where he found the journeys to and from school particularly problematic. He would walk a significant distance and rely on an infrequent bus service rather than travel home with a crowd of pupils. His form tutor remarked on how his isolation made him a vulnerable figure, especially on dark winter nights.

Confused attachment

Barrett and Trevitt (1991) describe confused attachment as one in which neither the parent nor the child have discovered a shared, fixed point, and give the impression of 'spinning within an uncontained space'. No contact seems possible and there is no apparent opportunity for the formulation of any attachment since the parent's emotional availability is inconsistent. The infant's behaviour appears to be excessively anxious. They may be offered tantalizing glimpses of closeness by their parent, only to have them instantly withdrawn. Both parent and infant seem to alternate between perpetual motion and sinking into deep despair. Whilst excessive activity can provide a defence against feelings of depression for some children, others may attempt to take control for themselves by adopting a parenting role.

The relationship between Roxana and her mother is an excellent example of confused attachment. As will be discussed in the subsequent case study (Chapter Seven), Roxana's mother suffers from extreme, and often unfounded, anxieties about her own health which border on hypochondria. Thus, whilst she seems genuinely concerned for Roxana's welfare, she lacks her own 'secure base' from which to offer Roxana support and security. For example, when Roxana was being bullied at school her mother was unable to talk through the situation and offer constructive support. Instead she assumed that Roxana was ill and took her to the doctor. In this way Roxana's mother appears to 'care for' her daughter but is clearly unable to deal appropriately with her practical and emotional needs.

Rejection

By comparison, as the term suggests, when a parent is unable to tolerate the child within their space this can result in rejection. In such a case it is difficult for the child to develop an idea of themselves as a valued individual, unless that is, they are able to develop a more positive interaction with an alternative attachment figure.

A rejecting parent is unable to be emotionally available for their child and consequently the child is unable to gain the reassurance, support and encouragement that are essential to them. The child's basic needs may be met but without reference to their feelings and they are therefore deprived of any meaningful interactions. Such children may direct all their energy towards trying to attract their parent's attention, although if this fails they may develop their own rejecting responses. As highlighted in a paper given by Lynne Murray at the 7th International Therapy Conference (1992), parental inability to respond appropriately to a child's attempts at communication may be thought of as a rejection of the child. Even with small babies the result can be that the child loses interest and stops trying to maintain contact with the parent.

Barrett and Trevitt (1991, p. 12) suggest that some children who have experienced rejecting parenting continue to avoid personal interaction and channel their energies into intensive scholastic learning. However, I would argue that such children may be rendered unable to learn effectively because of their underdeveloped sense of self-worth and inexperience of meaningful personal relationships. Whilst it might be relatively easy for class teachers to identify overprotective parenting it is difficult to observe rejecting parenting. This is due in part to the fact that 'rejecting' parents are less likely to visit school and show an active interest in their child. Moreover, given the 'common sentimentality surrounding motherhood' (Benjamin, 1990, p. 14), which dismisses or denies post-natal depression and rejection of children by mothers, it is likely that parents would hide or deny their rejecting behaviour even if they were aware of it.

Charlene is an example of a child rejected by her mother. Charlene's mother was an alcoholic with erratic and potentially violent mood swings. Consequently, whilst her mother was physically present in the family she may well have been frequently emotionally absent. An elder sister had assumed the parenting role within the family and a younger sibling had been adopted. According to Charlene, her younger brother had been adopted by a friend of the family and was being brought up as a cousin.

Charlene: Um, he is my proper brother but somebody else adopted him.
JC: I see. And so do you see him?
Charlene: Yeah. He doesn't ... he doesn't know about that um I'm his sister.

She sounded almost wistful when she commented that unlike her, he was living in a relatively affluent household and had 'everything he wants'. However, one can only speculate on the effect of finding out that one's siblings could be given away to others. Charlene's absence from school increased until finally it was realized that the family had in fact moved from the area without leaving a forwarding address.

What is clear from a discussion of these three kinds of anxious attachment is that insecure attachments in early childhood, or an inappropriate 'secure base' from which to explore the environment, can render children unable to learn. These 'learning disabled' children come to their teachers' attention not only because of their slow academic progress, but also because of their behaviour, which can range from disruptive acting out to total withdrawal. However, as withdrawal behaviour does not cause discipline problems for the teacher, it is likely that the child who withdraws will not receive the same level of attention as the potentially disruptive child.

Whilst an understanding of anxious attachments can help to explain pupil behaviour, as with the application of any psychological theories, care must be taken that such theories are not applied inappropriately or insensitively. Patterns of parenting are not simple predictors of possible behaviour. An individual's pattern of behaviour results from a unique response to specific circumstances. Moreover, as the case studies in the following chapter demonstrate, attachment behaviour is not the only cause of quiet withdrawn behaviour. Pupil behaviour in school is also likely to be affected by the pupils' perceptions of themselves and the learning task.

The effects of separation

Bowlby's account of attachment theory (1989b) highlights the need for parents to provide their children with an appropriate balance of separation and attachment. Implicit in this theory is the idea that sudden or prolonged separation from an attachment figure can be a major source of distress for a child. Whilst I accept that inappropriate or prolonged separation can cause distress, my work with habitually quiet non-participating children modifies Bowlby's account in two key ways. First, individuals differ considerably in their response to separation and in the way they are willing and able to discuss their feelings subsequently. Related to this is the notion that a lack of protest behaviour at the time of separation does not necessarily indicate an absence of distress. Secondly, by comparing the circumstances of children traumatized by separation with those who seem better able to cope with it or adjust to it, it is possible to highlight some of the factors which may influence different patterns of behaviour.

Different responses to separation

According to accounts offered by pupils and their parents, individuals differed considerably in the way they responded to separation from significant others, with responses varying from acute distress to relatively calm acceptance.

At one extreme Susie represents a child clearly traumatized by separation from her mother. Susie's father offers a graphic, if terse, account of the way in which she demonstrated her distress when her mother left home. 'Yes, she seemed right nervous. You'd just say summat to her and she'd jump, cringe back.' This suggests that during the early days of the separation from her mother Susie rejected her father's attempts to comfort or pacify her by physically moving away from him. Susie's feelings of insecurity at this time were possibly aggravated by the fact that the break with her mother was protracted. Susie was, and to a lesser extent still is, passed from mother to father. 'About first six months she didn't know

85

where she were. First she didn't want her and dumped her on me then she wanted her back, she were going off like that.' The terms in which her father discussed how she was moved from parent to parent must have left Susie in little doubt that there was a sense in which she was unwanted by either parent. One can only speculate on the anxieties generated in a young child by the experience of feeling unwanted, or at best tolerated, by the very people on whom she or he depends for survival. In Susie's case, her feelings of insecurity were probably heightened by constant changes of address and school which are of themselves unsettling.

Pamela exhibited similar distress on being separated from her father whilst he served a lengthy prison sentence. However, unlike Susie, Pamela became unusually clinging towards the remaining parent and would become extremely distressed whenever she realized that her mother was about to leave the house. Pamela's mother remembers that 'I couldn't, I wasn't allowed to go anywhere ... Pamela would stand up at the front door and I wasn't allowed to open it if she knew I was going somewhere without her'. Interestingly, her mother had not connected the change in Pamela's behaviour with her father's enforced absence from the family. However, Pamela's mother felt that the period of separation had negatively affected Pamela's relationship with her father. 'He had took himself away from her. So I think the closeness that they did have did drop quite a lot although it seems to come back now. But she did feel quite a lot of resentment towards him in the end 'cos he was away for quite a long while'.

Thus it can be seen that both Pamela and Susie were greatly distressed at being separated from parents in early childhood. This not only affected their relationships with their estranged parent but also influenced their relationships with those left to care for them. In addition I would argue that if their strategies of 'moving away from' and 'moving towards' others became habitual or rigid, this would in turn influence their future relationships.

Whilst some children exhibited distress during separation, a second group of children were described by their parents as well able to cope with separation from a parent or significant other. However, evidence acquired in interviews with the children concerned would suggest that the lack of protest behaviour, which was initially interpreted as acceptance, may well have indicated a deep distress. One example illustrates the point. Aberash associated her mother's return to work with her own loss of confidence. 'Sometimes she had to go to work, then I was a ... then when I had to go into the swimming baths again I was afraid to go in the water.' By comparison, her mother's account of the events suggests that Aberash was well able to cope with being left at nursery school. 'It was just a different environment from being at home with me that she knew and when I left her there it was fine ... She used to be upset when I came to collect her in the evening spoiling something that she obviously got into ... but she used to enjoy it.'

The distress that Aberash showed on her mother's return was explained by her mother as a response to having to leave something that she was enjoying rather than to 'anxiety or frustration' at being separated from her mother. Clearly Aberash and her mother offer conflicting accounts of the events. Given the guilt which mothers often feel in leaving the care of their children to others, Aberash's mother may have had an ulterior motive in wanting her version to be true. The fact that the mother later refers to the possible conflict between observable behaviour and 'anxiety' suggests that even she is not totally convinced by her own version of events. Subsequent interviews with Aberash confirmed the view that an absence of protest behaviour does not necessarily equate with an absence of distress at separation from a parent or significant other.

In sharp contrast, some children do seem to have been genuinely able to cope with parental separation. For example, neither Diana nor her sister were unduly traumatized by their mother's departure from the family home. Diana's father comments: 'It seems to work and they're all right, you know, they're quite happy. I don't think it's upset them that much actually.' He thought that this was due in part to the fact that they had unlimited access to their mother and that the home had become much calmer since he and his wife had stopped trying to live together. 'I think they prefer it to when we were living together 'cos we were always arguing, we couldn't have carried on you know.' The view that Diana had come to terms with her parents' divorce was largely borne out by remarks made by Diana herself. 'We see my mum every weekend, so nothing to really worry about.' The fact that both father and daughter talk about the divorce freely, between themselves and with others, suggests a degree of coming to terms with the situation. This relative openness is in sharp contrast to Susie's perpetual denial of events and feelings.

Factors which influence behaviour during separation

Evidence suggests that children differ considerably in their response to parental separation. At one extreme some children are greatly traumatized by events; other children are relatively able to adjust to and accept changing circumstances. An examination of the circumstances of separation suggests a number of factors which may influence how individuals respond to parental separation.

Of particular significance would seem to be the quality of the relationships which exist prior to separation both with the estranged parent and the remaining carer. In cases where individuals have suffered less trauma they have been able to sustain extremely close loving relationships with the remaining parent who was, or soon became, their 'prime attachment figure' or carer. For example, Diana expressed complete confidence in her remaining parent's ability to take care of her, both physically and emotionally. In such cases the child has an extremely close, warm and loving relationship with the remaining parent.

By comparison, both Pamela and Susie experienced separation from the parent who, for whatever reason, represented their closest relationship prior to separation. Whilst Pamela seems to have been sustained by her relationship with her mother, Susie seems to have rejected support from her father and to have had no 'secure base' on which she could depend. Similarly Aberash, who spent a great deal of her early childhood with a series of childminders, may have felt rejected by her mother as she was passed from person to person. In all cases separation from their primary attachment figure may well have affected relationships with both the remaining and the estranged parent. Moreover, the perceived lack of a secure base may well have negatively affected these individuals' feelings of self-worth and made them timid of entering into relationships with others. This could help to explain their seeming reluctance to talk freely with pupils and teachers in school.

Close attachment to the remaining parent or significant other is one possible factor which might contribute to an individual's ability to cope with separation in early childhood. Another factor might well be related to the nature of the separation. Where the separation is unclear or protracted, as in the case of Susie who was still unsettled after a number of years, this is likely to compound rather than alleviate distress. In cases where children appear to have suffered less trauma the conditions of their parents' separation have been clear almost from the outset. For example, neither Diana nor her sister seem to have any doubt as to their relationship with their estranged parent. Incidentally, as both Diana's and Pamela's experiences demonstrate, this primary attachment figure and 'the person who understands me best of all' can be the father, which underlies the importance of fathers in the lives of individual children, as highlighted by post-feminist accounts of parenting (see, for example, Chodorow, 1978 and Benjamin, 1990).

The presence of step-parents and stepchildren may well be a contributory factor in the extent to which individuals are able to come to terms with parental separation. This is invariably related to the need to share their parents' time and affection with others. However, such jealousy is not restricted to stepfamilies: all the children who lived with siblings expressed some feelings of jealousy towards others who seemed at times to have more than their fair share of parental attention or material goods.

A fourth important factor which may influence an individual's behaviour is the degree to which they feel able and willing to discuss both the circumstances of the separation and the possibly conflicting feelings which were generated as a result. Related to this is the need to understand the difficulties which excessively quiet children have in expressing such feelings and in particular the strategies which such pupils adopt that might prevent them from being heard. In extreme cases there may be a need for trained educational therapists or counsellors to be available in schools to help children to explore such unresolved issues.

Within the context of the interviews pupils found it necessary or desirable to acknowledge that they had experienced some form of separation or loss within their own families. However, the way in which some pupils introduced and discussed the subject suggests that they are still in the process of coming to terms with the events and their feelings. Such pupils clearly need time to discuss their feelings and may well benefit from some form of counselling with a trusted adult. Without such support the issues remain unresolved and could well 'get in the way' of positive learning relationships in school.

This evidence suggests that the conditions in which children experience separation from attachment figures are as important as the separation itself. The factors which influence an individual's ability to cope with separation are summarized by Nancy Chodorow (1978, p. 75). She speculates that separation is not of itself harmful to children and where children do suffer it is in situations associated with 'sudden separation from their primary caretaker, major family crisis or disruption in their life, inadequate interaction with those caretakers they do have, or with so many caretakers that the child cannot form a growing and ongoing bond with a small number of people'. The acknowledgement that it is the quality of care which is important, not that it be provided by a biological mother, has clear implications for parenting and childcare.

An understanding of parent–child relationships can help

teachers to understand the underlying causes of much of the non-participatory behaviour they witness in school. In addition, an appreciation of the need for both separation and connectedness in relationships has implications for the quality of relationships in school. If difficulty with interpersonal relationships is the cause of quiet withdrawn behaviour, then relationships which offer appropriate levels of security and challenge must lie at the heart of effective teaching and learning. The development of relationships which encourage dialogue in schools is central to providing an appropriate learning environment for all pupils. However, the need for appropriate levels of separation and connectedness in relationships (between teachers and pupils and among peers) is particularly acute for quiet pupils already silenced by anxious or deviant attachments with parents or significant others.

6 The nature of the family

In the previous chapter I commented on the connection between the nature of parent–child relationships and the quality of relationships in school. Throughout the chapter I used attachment theory to describe the ways in which parent–child relationships can shape children's perceptions of themselves and also influence subsequent relationships with teachers and peers in school. However, I also made it clear that I rejected some of the assumptions about family life which have come to be synonymous with attachment theory. For example, I do not accept the belief that fathers cannot become primary attachment figures for their children. Nor do I accept the idea that lone-parent families or stepfamilies cannot provide secure relationships for children. In this chapter I review selected literature to support my argument that what really matters is the quality of the parent–child relationship, not the sex of the parent or the structure of the family.

Literature on early childhood relationships tends to assume that women have prime, or sole, responsibility for the care of children. In examining the changing role of fathers I begin by discussing why women mother. I explore the basis of this assumption and the extent to which it contributes to an under-standing of what is meant by the terms 'mother' and 'father'. This leads me to a discussion of the changing role of fathers and the possible benefits of shared parenting for both parents and children. The notion of fathers as providers of nurturing care is developed in a discussion of non-traditional families, specifically lone-parents and stepfamilies. Throughout the chapter I explore the view that traditional 'male' and 'female' parenting roles are socially constructed rather than innate. In this chapter I argue that it is the quality of parent care, not the sex of the parent, which is fundamental to an individual's psychological and emotional development.

Why women mother

The assumption that women care for children permeates much of the work on early childhood relationships (Arcana, 1981; Benjamin, 1990; Nice, 1992; Rich, 1992). For example, Nancy Chodorow began *The Reproduction of Mothering* (1978, p. 3) with the assertion that women not only bear children but that they also 'take primary responsibility for infant care ... and sustain primary emotional ties with infants'. She is not alone in assuming that when biological mothers do not parent, other women, rather than men, virtually always take their place (Apter, 1985; Smith, 1990). This appears to preclude the possibility of fathers providing primary care for their children.

Two arguments are put forward to justify the connection between women and mothering. The first is 'biological determinism', which suggests that women are predisposed to mother by their biological experience of menstruation and childbirth. The second argument is that girls are taught to care for children by their experience of being mothered by women. The two views are not necessarily mutually exclusive and a nature–nurture debate continues, even among feminists, and is itself fraught with contradictions and ambiguities.

Some writers, such as Chodorow (1978), acknowledge the influence of biological experiences, but also maintain the importance of the sociological and psychological determinants of gender and of mothering. Thus Chodorow concluded her chapter 'Why women mother' by stating that 'Women's capacities for mothering and their abilities to get gratification from it are strongly internalised and psychologically enforced, and are built developmentally into the feminine psychic structure' (p. 39). Her premise is that women are prepared psychologically for mothering through the developmental situation in which they grow up, mothered by women. By comparison, men do not identify with their mothers and consequently do not develop, or (even worse) repress, any predetermination to nurture which they may have.

However, whilst Chodorow confidently plays down the connection between biological experience and motherhood, the alternative viewpoint has recently been strengthened by the work of psychotherapist Alessandra Piontelli (1992). In a longitudinal study described in *From Fetus to Child*, Piontelli describes her observations of the behaviour of several children from a very early stage in the womb using ultrasound scans, through birth, to infancy and childhood. This study is the first of its kind and therefore her findings cannot be verified. However, as her findings suggest a 'remarkable continuity of behaviour before and after birth' (p. ix), this could be cited as evidence of a strong and unique attachment between mother and child. Certainly her work with sets of twins supports the view that their relationship is formed in the womb. Replication of this work would involve overcoming the ethical issue connected with extensive use of ultrasound and its possible effect on the developing fetus.

Other writers such as Jenny Morris (1992) cite the actual experiences of women, in celebrating the special relationship between mother and child which begins with childbirth. For some mothers the moment of birth is seen as a joyful and overwhelming experience which is associated with 'a huge, unconditional, mutual love' (p. 6). However, positive experiences of childbirth are not universal, nor are nurturing or 'maternal' instincts limited to women. Post-natal depression and rejection of children by their mother are often dismissed or denied by the 'common sentimentality surrounding motherhood' (Benjamin, 1990, p. 14). Moreover, work by Stein Braten (1992) on the relationship formed between a father and his premature daughter confirms that some men, at least, are capable of nurturing relationships with very small children. His work suggests that increasing parental involvement may require little more than a change of attitude on the part of medical staff and parents. To what extent such a change of attitude may be regarded as desirable is a separate issue, which will be discussed in the section focusing on shared parenting.

The nature–nurture debate is an important aspect of the parenting debate and as such represents a fundamental dilemma. If 'mothering' is learned rather than innate, or conversely if nurturing is seen as a universal human characteristic, then there is no reason for precluding fathers from caring for their children. Moreover, if relationships with children are rewarding and fulfilling then fathers are being deprived if they do not have the opportunity to spend some time with, and get to know, their children. Yet many women do not wish to deny the special relationships they feel they have with their children through their experiences of pregnancy and childbirth. In addition, shared parenting and childcare have serious implications for patterns of employment. There is no consensus on the issue of the employment of mothers outside the home. Some women choose to work in order to maintain their independence and careers; others are forced to work by financial considerations.

Some writers feel that providing childcare and maintaining an independent identity are not mutually exclusive. In her account of mothering, Jessica Benjamin expresses a wish that the mother maintain her independent identity, whilst having total responsibility for the care of her child. Benjamin stresses the need to view the mother as a subject in her own right, 'principally because of contemporary feminism, which made us aware of the disastrous results for women of being reduced to the mere extension of a two-month-old' (1990, p. 23). Sadly, she does not discuss how this might be achieved.

The issue of 'mothering' is further complicated by the fact that the term 'to mother' has come to include care and support of men. 'Women of all classes are now expected to nurture and support husbands in addition to providing them with food and a clean house' (Chodorow, 1978, p. 5). There can be an unbreachable line between public and private values which rests on 'the tacit assumption that women will continue to

95

preserve and protect personal life, the task to which they have been assigned' (Benjamin, 1990, p. 197). As Terri Apter (1985) implied when she called her book *Why Women Don't Have Wives*, women are held responsible for caring, not only for their children but also for their husbands.

However, this care is often ignored or undervalued. Carol Gilligan (1982, p. 17) argued that while women have taken care of men, men have, in 'their theories of psychological development, as in their economic arrangements, tended to assume or devalue that care'. The physical care which women provide is to some extent overt and quantifiable; women do the bulk of household chores. Emotional care is more difficult to quantify; it takes the form of supportive listening, ego-stroking and ego-building, approval and support (Cline and Spender, 1987). Moreover, girls are taught or encouraged (depending on the view of socialization adopted), to do this from a very early age.

Caring for others, especially children, is an important task which, even now, has a low status in our society. This contradiction is part of the dilemma inherent in assigning parental roles. The following section examines the roles of mothers and fathers and discusses to what extent these roles are changing.

The difference between 'mothering' and 'fathering'

In many ways the terms 'mothering' and 'fathering' mean something very different. One fundamental difference is that, when fathers take an active part in caring for their children they do so from choice; by comparison, when women 'mother' they are fulfilling a socially prescribed role (Smith, 1990). The assumption that women 'mother' means that a mother's absence from her children is less acceptable and more harshly judged than the absence of the father. Moreover, the terms are not interchangeable. Whilst in some circumstances a father may be described as 'mothering' his child, a mother is never thought of as 'fathering' her children, 'even in the rare societies in which a high ranking woman may take a wife and be the social father of her wife's children' (Chodorow, 1978,

p. 11). Incidentally, this reference to 'high ranking women' suggests that, while it is reasonably acceptable for women in high status positions to leave the care of their children to others, it is less acceptable for women of low status. This has serious implications for women's role in the job market, irrespective of whether they are there by choice or necessity. Whilst men may automatically leave the care of their children to others, women are criticized for doing the same, unless doing so enables them to earn a high salary or make a major contribution to society.

However, June Statham (1986, p. 11) argue that the second half of the 1970s saw a rise in the image of the involved father 'given, naturally, the constraints imposed by their full-time job outside the home'. According to Statham, the term 'fathering' is acquiring a new meaning. While originally it referred only to *being* the biological father and did not require a man to actually *do* anything (beyond his role in conception), it is coming to be used in a similar way to the word 'mothering'. Similarly, she suggests that the verb 'to parent' is finding its way into the English language, apparently in response to a felt need for a term that could apply to tasks that both parents do.

In *Reassessing Fatherhood* (1987) Charles Lewis coined the term 'new father' to describe a man who is both highly nurturant to his children and increasingly involved in their care and the housework. However, he cautions that, 'despite a wave of optimism driving contemporary accounts, the evidence for the existence of such a man is much less convincing' (Lewis and O'Brien, 1987, p. 1). There is evidence to suggest that the majority of fathers who live with their children do not take responsibility for childcare. Nevertheless, nurturing fathers do exist; indeed, two out of the twelve children featured in this book were cared for by their fathers following parental separation and divorce. However, it has to be acknowledged that there might be a tendency in some theoretical studies to overestimate paternal involvement in childcare simply because 'it is judged against the expectation of non-involvement, child

97

raising being seen as basically a mother's responsibility' (Statham, 1986, p. 15).

Vivien Nice (1992) claims that, whilst responsibility for childcare rests with women, legal anomalies ensure paternal rights over the child. She maintains that 'the basic tenet of current patriarchy is that mothers are merely carriers of male seed, and only fathers are related to their children' (p. 3). As evidence she cites the laws relating to paternal inheritance and the contemporary use of mothers as 'surrogates'. This is an extreme view which fails to acknowledge the anger and frustration fathers experience when they are separated from their children and denied access (McCormack, 1990). The issue of paternal rights and responsibilities is a difficult and emotive subject. Only time will tell how effective the 1989 Children Act will be in clarifying anomalies of law such as those raised by the Baby M case, quoted by Phyllis Chester in *Sacred Bond* (1990).

Legal anomalies aside, an increase in paternal involvement in childcare does not necessarily indicate that women feel free from maternal ties. The connection between maternal separation and deprivation is longstanding and permeates much that is written on early childhood relationships. Consequently, maternal separation is continually linked with guilt for the mother, and suffering – even deprivation – for the child. This is true even when the separation is brief and childcare is assumed by a known and trusted adult. Developmental theories that focus exclusively upon maternal influences are one factor which forms a major barrier to genuine shared parenting. Other possible conceptual barriers to shared parenting may include stereotypic conceptions of family roles and an underestimation of a young child's ability to adapt to a number of social relationships (Pederson, 1980).

The following section examines the possible effects of shared parenting on both parents and children.

Shared parenting

The emphasis of this section is that, whilst many and varied claims have been made for and against the notion of shared parenting, these may not equate with actual experience and are not necessarily borne out by research findings. This section addresses the claims made for shared parenting by Christiane Olivier and by Nancy Chodorow. It then compares these claims with research evidence provided by a team of three workers featured in *Reassessing Fatherhood* (1987) edited by Charles Lewis and Margaret O'Brien.

Christiane Olivier (1989) bases her defence of shared parenting, and a related fear of lone parenting, on a negative view of the mother–child relationship. She argues that both boys and girls need their fathers in order to counter the negative, even dangerous, effects of mothers. According to Olivier, girls have a negative relationship with their mothers and, especially as they reach adolescence, actively fight against any tendency to become like them. Thus, she describes an adolescent need for independent identity in the negative terms of 'mother-hating', a very different account of the relationship to that portrayed by Terri Apter (1985). Olivier feels that sole parenting by women is equally damaging to sons, as there is a danger that the all-powerful mother lives with her son without any male images to break up his dangerous one-to-one relationship. 'Not only do we have the absent father; we also have the permanently present mother' (p. 131). Thus Olivier denies the extremely powerful masculine influences portrayed by society, and through the media, which counteract the effects of women trying to rear their sons in a non–sexist way (Arcana, 1983). Her negative view of the mother–child relationship leads Olivier to argue for shared parenting and against lone parenting by women, 'in spite of the express wishes of some of them, and against what men believe' (p. 9). Moreover, she envisages the need for a 'new man' who will not only father a 'new son' capable of independence from his mother, but who will also father a 'new daughter' who, right from the moment of birth, will have an adequate 'sexual object'.

Interestingly, Olivier begins her chapter on 'The Family' with a quote from David Cooper: 'We don't need mother and father any more. We only need mothering and fathering' (p. 130). This implies that the roles of mothering and fathering can be carried out by parents of either sex and that either mothers or fathers can be adequate parents for their children. However, she does not develop this theme. Instead she draws attention to the difficulty of adopting non-traditional roles. Despite wishing to be involved in the care of their children, fathers are excluded from physical connectedness to their children by mothers who 'keep the child to themselves' (p. 135). She does however acknowledge the emergence of a new kind of woman: one who wants to live *with* her child not *through* it. Such a woman wants to be socially active even when she has young children. Yet, as Olivier admits, childcare provision is woefully lacking, even if the mother can overcome the guilt which society expects her to feel at leaving her child to the care of others.

Nancy Chodorow (1978) leaves the subject of equal or shared parenting to the end of her book where it appears rather as an afterthought. Her general thesis is that in a number of ways shared parenting would ensure increased social equality. However, she is vague as to exactly how this might be achieved. She stated that equal parenting would not threaten anyone's primary sense of gendered self but admits

> Nor do we know what this self would look like in a non-sexist society ... Anyone who has good primary relationships has the foundation for nurturance and love, and women would retain these even as men would gain them. Men would be able to retain the autonomy which comes from differentiation without that differentiation being rigid and reactive, and women would have more opportunity to gain it. People's sexual choices might become more flexible, less desperate. (p. 218)

Her expectation is that equal parenting would blur gender differences by giving both men and women the positive capacities associated with people of the opposite sex. This contradicts the view that shared parenting would not threaten a primary sense of gendered self. Surely, if men and women acquired the good characteristics traditionally associated with the opposite sex then gender differences cease to have any meaning? Moreover, what is there to stop individuals acquiring negative characteristics as well as positive ones? One criticism often levelled at women who have achieved success in male-dominated public spheres is that they have done so by forfeiting traditional female characteristics.

Chodorow particularly stresses the effect which shared parenting may have on the development of boys. She maintained that for boys identification processes and masculine role learning are not likely to be embedded in relationships with their fathers or men, but rather involve 'the denial of affective relationships to their mothers' (p. 177). Consequently, boys who develop their sense of self in opposition to the mother establish more rigid ego boundaries and often a defensive denigration of that which is feminine or associated with the mother. Thus, Chodorow identified men's fear of the pre-Oedipal mother, and of losing their sense of masculinity, as fuelling male dominance in society. In this way she developed Karen Horney's thesis that a masculine contempt for and devaluation of women is a manifestation of a deeper 'dread of women'. 'A masculine fear and terror of maternal omnipotence that arises as one major consequence of their early caretaking and socialisation by women' (p. 183).

However, in *Public Man, Private Women* (1981) Jean Elshtain expresses concern over Chodorow's notion that male parenting would change the male stance towards women. Benjamin (1990) links this to the 'preconscious assumption' that men would raise their children with the 'same impersonal rationality that they display in public enterprise' leading to a 'fear of being left in the father's care' (p. 204). The connection between a psychoanalytic model and social or political change is not self-evident, and it is not clear, for example, that shared parenting is a completely adequate response to patriarchal structures.

Whilst shared parenting may not be sufficient to overturn patriarchal structures, it is not of itself harmful to children. Chodorow quoted research which supported the view that children do not suffer from multiple parenting or shared childcare. She maintained that where children do suffer is in multiple parenting situations associated with 'sudden separation from their primary caretaker, major family crisis or disruption in their life, inadequate interaction with those caretakers they do have, or with so many caretakers that the child cannot form a growing and ongoing bond with a small number of people' (p. 75). Thus it is acknowledged that it is the quality of care which is important, not that it be provided by a biological mother. This significantly qualifies attachment theories as proposed by Bowlby (1989a, 1989b).

In *Reassessing Fatherhood* (1987) Michael Lamb and his colleagues examined the influence of a 'change to more egalitarian parental and occupational roles on the family' (p. 109). They considered the losses and gains for men and women in shared parenting and presented a broad spectrum of issues which must be considered when attempting to understand greater paternal involvement in childcare. Not surprisingly, given the complex issues involved, they concluded that there was little evidence that increased paternal involvement has any clear-cut or direct effects. They felt that paternal involvement could only be understood in the context of individual families, and as such, it was misguided to see increased paternal involvement as a universally desirable goal. They preferred that 'attempts should be made to increase the options available to fathers, so that those who want to be can become more involved in their children's lives' (p. 109). Thus the fathering role is seen in terms of paternal choice rather than socially prescribed roles. Presumably, an increase in the number of men choosing to care for their children may in turn affect the extent to which paternal care assumes the status of 'socially prescribed role'.

One of the possible advantages of shared parenting for fathers is thought to be closer, richer and more enjoyable personal relationships between fathers and children. However, Lamb *et al.* cautioned against such an interpretation. They considered that there was insufficient evidence to conclude that 'involvement produced sensitivity and competence rather than that the more competent and sensitive fathers choose to become more involved' (p. 118). The assertion that only competent and sensitive fathers choose to care for their children seems reasonable but it is difficult to verify. Moreover, many fathers who had been prime caretakers had fairly negative perceptions of their experiences. These fathers 'felt deprived of adult contacts and they found their lives boring and repetitive' (p. 120). This is perhaps an experience shared by many mothers.

A negative aspect of shared parenting is that women may find it difficult to relinquish the care of their children, especially if they feel that due to a lack of experience these responsibilities are 'being fulfilled by others less vigorously (or at least differently) than they would like' (Lamb *et al.*, 1987, p. 122). Even when the mother feels that the father provides adequate childcare he may neglect the housework which the mother feels is an integral part of the 'mothering' role. More seriously, another possible consequence of increased paternal involvement is that it may diminish, or even eliminate, maternal domination in the child-rearing role. Some women may well resent this 'both because of its effects on the marital power balance as well as because it may dilute and make less exclusive mother–child relationships' (p. 122). Thinking in terms of social equality, agreeing to share childcare may facilitate women's opportunities to work and have a career. However, there is the risk that they may leave themselves without an arena in which they dominate. Similarly, by choosing to be involved in the care of their children, men may have to relinquish career status or advancement. Thus, increased parental involvement could influence employment patterns and practices, such as job- sharing and paternity leave. Yet it has to be remembered that not all parents are employed, and of those who are many will not have careers where such changes in employment practice are likely to be possible.

On balance, and for a variety of reasons, shared parenting tends to be viewed as a potentially positive move towards greater social equality for parents. It is also viewed as an opportunity for children of both sexes to experience closeness and separation in relationships with both men and women. This may influence not only their relationships with other people, but also the way in which they come to regard themselves and the roles they choose to adopt. However, changing from a traditional family to a more egalitarian one is a difficult process with inherent tensions and difficulties. The idea that what matters is the quality of nurturing care which children receive, not that it is provided by the biological mother, is continued in the following section which examines other non-traditional family patterns such as those adopted by lone and step-parents.

Other non-traditional families

'There is now no single British family but a rich variety of forms, states, traditions, norms and usages' (Laslett, 1982, p. xii). Moreover, it is important to regard lone parents and their children as households and families in their own right, and not as a mutant form of the so-called 'normal' two-parent family. Unless, and until, belief in the cultural 'normality' of the two-parent family is suspended, there will be a stigma attached to non-traditional families, and such families will be condemned to unfavourable comparison. This section examines two examples of non-traditional parenting, namely lone parenting and step-parenting.

Lone parenting
The routes to lone parenting are many and varied. Moreover, as each individual's experience is unique it is meaningless to think in terms of a 'typical' lone parent. Whilst the majority of parents come to lone parenting through separation, divorce, or the

death of a partner, an increasing number of women are actively choosing it (Morris, 1992). However, there is evidence to suggest that this route to lone parenting is primarily a middle-class choice (Renvoize, 1985). For lesbians, becoming single mothers by choice may be 'a very significant step forward in forming their identity' (Leonard and Speakman, 1986, p. 60). In broad terms, lone parents occupy a marginal position in contemporary British society. They are marginalized by financial considerations. Lone parents are more likely than other parents to be trying to survive on state benefits or low wages (Glendenings and Millar, 1987). Moreover, low incomes may also imply poor housing: 'In both a tenural and a geographical sense, lone-parent households are concentrated in the poorer parts of the urban system' (Hardey and Crow, 1991, p. 47).

In addition lone parents occupy a marginal position in social life, being effectively excluded from full participation in mainstream activities 'by the couple-centred "family" ideology which permeates the social structure' (Hardey and Crow, 1991, p. 1). Sandra Shaw (1991) in her study of Sheffield women emphasized that the specific loneliness experienced by lone parents is the loneliness of not having a partner, implying that this was different to the need for another parent for their children. She drew attention to the role of support groups in providing a social outlet for both parents and children, as well as practical and emotional support. Family and friends were also seen as an invaluable source of support. Similarly, Margaret O'Brien (1987) identified different patterns of kinship and friendships among lone fathers as compared with married fathers. She suggested that, whilst single fathers occupy an ambivalent role in society, the fact that they have moved into the private domain of home and childcare opens up 'for men the possibility of closer relationships of a different kind with women' (p. 242).

One consequence of regarding two parents as the 'norm' is that lone parents are often portrayed as powerless victims of social disadvantage, thus reinforcing the stereotypical image of lone parents as dependent. Against this background it is easy for lone parents who are poor to be mistakenly perceived as 'poor parents', just as lone parents are also especially vulnerable to the label 'problem families'. One of the major criticisms of lone parenting has been that children, especially boys, are likely to be negatively affected by the absence of their father (Pirani, 1989; Olivier, 1989). However, Stephen Collins (1991) finds no evidence to support the link between lone parenting and delinquency. While he admits that there is evidence of a higher than average rate of delinquency among children of divorced parents, he does not find evidence of any 'necessary shortcomings in the emotional lives of lone-parent households' (p. 161). Instead he links an increase in delinquency to the pain and uncertainty of divorce, poverty, and a bias against lone parent families within the judicial system. Thus it could be that what may be regarded as mere high spirits is thought of as delinquent when the child is known to come from a one-parent family. This is difficult to confirm from Stephen Collins's work as he does not offer a definition of delinquency.

Whilst it is often the negative aspects of lone parenting which are stressed there are positive aspects. These include not having to care for a partner, which could be viewed as reducing the household chores that have to be performed, financial independence and control, as well as the emotional gains which 'can be seen to revolve around ideas of independence, pride and self-esteem, confidence, and a feeling of doing a hard job (that is, parenting) well' (Shaw, 1991, p. 147).

Vivien Nice (1992) also recognizes that single parenting may have benefits. She suggests that a mother without a male partner may actually be at an advantage 'as she does not have to continually balance the needs of children and partner, and she may feel freer to seek the support and companionship of female friends or relatives without being accused of disloyalty' (p. 31). However, in considering lone parenting it must be remembered that, in common with the rest of the population, parents are likely to hold contradictory views about their situation. Thus an individual may be aware of both the positive and negative aspects of being a lone parent.

Step-parents

Work on divorced families and stepfamilies tends to be descriptive rather than analytical. Moreover, accounts of actual lived experience often explode commonly held beliefs. One such example is Ann Mitchell's (1985) interviews with children who had experienced parental divorce. This study contradicts the commonly held view that children are happier if their parents separate than if they continue to live in a family where the parents argue or fight. Similarly, the notion that fathers are not affected by being separated from their children is contradicted by the work of Mary McCormack (1990). She uses personal accounts to testify to the pain and anger which fathers can feel when they lose contact with their children.

On the subject of stepfamilies Donna Smith (1990) emphasizes that the relationships between women and stepchildren may be different from those experienced by other kinds of mothers, such as those who foster or adopt. There is no reason to suppose that this does not also hold true for stepfathers. Foster parents and parents who adopt are seeking fulfilment through the care of children, whilst by comparison, stepparents are seeking fulfilment through an adult relationship. 'Stepchildren may add to the richness of relationship ... but that is seldom the primary reason for entering the relationship' (Smith, 1990, p. 25). In so far as a step-parent is outside the relationship between the child and its natural parent the steprelationship can be strained, and there can be hostility, perhaps based on jealousy, between the adults and the children.

The role of step-parent, in common with all other forms of parenting, is fraught with contradictions and preconceptions. Children come to school with assumptions of parenting based on their own experiences. It is important that teachers accept the children's experiences whilst fostering tolerance of other forms of parenting. Similarly, teachers should be aware of how their own assumptions about parents and families could colour their expectations of the children they teach.

Psychoanalytic interpretations are based on some essential truths which equate with actual experience. However, there is

107

a danger that these experiences can be manipulated to fit a theory which then becomes the received and accepted truth. When the theory and the experience do not equate, the tendency is to deny the experience. For example, many, perhaps all, women will recognize and relate to the idea of the 'little girl within' (Eichenbaum and Orbach, 1985). It is then only a short step to believing that this 'little girl' exists because of inadequacies in our relationship with our mothers.

These accounts of parenting challenge previously held assumptions that only mothers can nurture children. The suggestion that traditional male and female roles are constructed, rather than inherent, leads naturally to the notion that fathers can take an active role in the nurturing of their children. The suggestion that individuals benefit from acknowledging both the male and female aspects of their personality leads to an acceptance of one-parent families as viable family units. An examination of issues of separation and connectedness in parent–child relationships has clear implications for parents. However, what I would like to emphasize here is the possible implications for teachers working with quiet withdrawn pupils in mainstream classrooms.

I believe that an understanding of separation and connectedness as portrayed by post-feminist accounts of parenting should lead teachers to re-examine the quality of their relationships with parents. In particular teachers should examine the ways in which stereotypical views, which regard nuclear two-parent families as the 'norm', may exclude or marginalize fathers and lone parents. A re-examination of the parenting role should also influence the ways in which parents are portrayed in school. It is important that textbooks and other teaching materials do not portray lone-parent families as a mutant form of the so-called 'normal' two-parent family. Similarly, teachers should be aware of how their own assumptions about parents and families could colour their expectations of the children they teach.

An understanding of the complementary nature of separation and connectedness in relationships should also lead teachers to re-examine the nature of their relationships with pupils. I believe that an appropriate balance of separation and connectedness is important for all pupils. However, being able to relate to, and feel connected with, teachers and peers may be a crucial precursor to learning for those pupils already silenced by what they perceive to be anxiety in relationships. My experience as both a teacher and a researcher suggests that successful teachers are those who recognize the importance of pupils and teachers bringing their 'authentic loving selves' to the learning relationship.

7 Three illustrative case studies

This chapter expands and develops the themes raised in the previous two chapters by applying them to three individual case studies. The first of these identifies a clear link between Roxana's seemingly erratic behaviour in school and the nature of her relationship with her mother. It illustrates how knowledge of Roxana's 'confused' attachment with her mother could help teachers to provide appropriate support for Roxana during times of acute anxiety in school.

By comparison, the second case study illustrates how an understanding of Aberash's relationship with her mother offers only a partial explanation of Aberash's acute withdrawal from the social and academic life of the classroom. There is evidence to suggest that frequent separation from her mother has affected Aberash's ability and willingness to form and sustain relationships in school. However, Aberash and her mother suggest that incipient racism in the British educational system prevents black children from taking an active role in their education. Certainly, racial differences between home and school may affect relationships between Aberash and her predominantly white teachers and peers. Significantly, it was during lengthy conversations with Aberash's mother outside school that the subject of racism was introduced.

The third study also highlights the way in which 'in-school factors' can contribute to the incidence of quiet non-participatory behaviour. Diana has a secure relationship with her father and appears to be adjusting well to her parents' separation. Thus there appears to be no link between Diana's quiet non-participatory behaviour and the quality of her early rela-

110

tionships with her parents. Diana's withdrawal in the classroom seems to originate from her inability to form relationships with her teacher and her view that 'good pupils' are passive and compliant. It is tempting to link Diana's refusal to see herself as worthy of the teacher's time and attention with her perception of herself as a working-class girl, destined to fulfil the socially prescribed role of wife and mother.

Case Study One: Roxana: silenced by anxiety

I have already established that much of the quiet behaviour witnessed in school has its origins in early parent–child relationships. Consequently, I begin this case study with an account of Roxana's behaviour in school. A subsequent account of the nature of her relationship with her mother helps to explain her erratic behaviour in school and suggest ways in which teachers may support her in overcoming her anxieties.

Roxana's behaviour in school

Roxana's behaviour in school was erratic as she appeared to swing from quiet confidence to total despair. Whilst at times her behaviour seemed to be the epitome of confident self-assurance, at others she seemed to come psychically 'undone' at the mere thought of what might happen. I will refer to two specific incidents.

The first occurred during Roxana's final year in primary school. During a tape-recorded interview Roxana was asked how she would improve the small group discussions in which she took part. She appeared to have given some thought to the subject and spoke passionately about the need for an opportunity to work as a member of mixed-sex groups. She saw this as a positive way to break down barriers of communication between the boys and girls in the class. In the context of the interview we explored the idea and tried to anticipate how such co-operation might be achieved. However, a few days later, when the opportunity came for her to work in mixed-sex groups Roxana refused to participate. What separates her inability to take part from a simple case of 'cold feet' is the seemingly total despair which she exhibited. She stood at the edge of the room literally shaking with fear and clearly extremely close to tears. It was almost as if working with individuals who were not her close and trusted friends somehow threatened her very existence.

The speed with which Roxana appeared to shift from confidence to total despair is illustrated by the second example, which occurred during her first year at secondary school. The lesson was music, her favourite. During the first part of the lesson Roxana appeared to be a confident and able pupil. Looking happy and self-assured, she moved easily from instrument to instrument, carrying out the teacher's instructions. Moreover, she taught other pupils, both boys and girls, how to play. Indeed, her confidence seemed to grow as her suggestions as to how the music should progress were accepted by the teacher.

However, as the composition of the music neared completion and the class prepared for a 'performance' in front of another class Roxana's behaviour suddenly changed. Her countenance became sullen and unhappy. She fidgeted nervously with her fingers, and seemed prepared to become part of the audience. After an irritable comment from her teacher that she was 'being silly' she consented to take part, which amounted to nothing more than unenthusiastic tapping of a tambourine. Throughout the rest of the lesson she stood close to the classroom wall attempting to hide behind her fringe, seemingly on the verge of tears. Whatever had prompted the change of behaviour, it is not too dramatic to describe the effect as devastating.

A striking feature of this incident was the teacher's obvious irritation at Roxana's violent and seemingly wilful change of mood. When she opted out of the music lesson the teacher responded with annoyance, bordering on anger, that an obviously talented musician should choose to become temperamental at a time when he was under pressure himself. If such behaviour is seen as wilful defiance, this is clearly challenging to the teacher's authority. As Roxana's former teacher I could identify with his frustration, as I also wanted her to be seen to do well in her new school.

However, if pupils like Roxana are to be educated in mainstream school and have access to the full curriculum and social life of the school, her seemingly erratic behaviour needs to be understood, not merely tolerated. Observation of Roxana over several years and in a variety of situations suggests that her sudden withdrawal was not wilful defiance but rather a defence mechanism to protect herself from being overwhelmed by what she perceived to be external threats. In many respects Roxana's frequent and dramatic shifts of mood in response to relatively minor events illustrate a need to 'preserve her existence' in the face of overwhelming anxieties. This raises two important and interrelated issues. First, to what extent is Roxana's experience of acute anxiety and inability to cope related to her early relationships with her parents? Secondly, how would an understanding of Roxana's relationship with her mother help teachers to offer appropriate support in the classroom?

Roxana's relationship with her mother

When asked 'Who is the most important person in your life?', Roxana said, without hesitation, her mother. Except for noting the time her father left home to set up house with his pregnant girlfriend, Roxana hardly mentioned her father. Consequently, her father appears to be a distant figure who did not take an active role in the life of his family. Roxana's lack of relationship with her father could well help to explain her extraordinary interest in older boys. It certainly goes some way to explain her extremely close overprotective relationship with her mother.

As has already been said, evidence gathered from interviews with both mother and daughter suggests that theirs was a relationship based on confused attachment. This is a relationship in which neither the parent nor the child seems to have discovered a shared, fixed point and they seem to be spinning together within an uncontained space. For me, this kind of relationship is one in which mother and daughter are held together but apart by a force which prevents total separation or greater intimacy.

An interview with Roxana's mother soon revealed that she was an extremely anxious woman who was preoccupied with a fear of ill-health which bordered on hypochondria. Not only did she perceive herself to be suffering from a number of mysterious and incurable medical problems, she also anticipated medical problems for Roxana. A good example of anxiety leading to overprotectiveness was when she took Roxana – 'a hyperactive child' – to the doctor for his advice. She was surprised to find that his advice for dealing with a child who would not settle to sleep at night was simply to leave her alone. Although she admits that this was a difficult thing to do, it had in fact 'cured' Roxana within a relatively short time.

Anxiety for her daughter's health led to several trips to the doctor over issues which turned out to have no medical basis. The most serious of these – one which had a direct influence on Roxana's education – was during a spate of severe bullying by a particular boy in her class. Roxana's mother recalled how Roxana had become extremely distressed at the mere sight of the boy: 'Getting right timid again. You know, as if she was frightened to death of him.' Typically, she had previously assumed that the change in Roxana's behaviour was caused by a serious medical condition. 'In fact she's got a photo upstairs which she had took at that time when she was ill and the bones here are just sticking out of her face, she looked really ill. In fact I thought she had got leukaemia because she was just losing weight terrible.'

It is probably significant that despite her over-anxiety, Roxana's mother was not close enough to Roxana to find out the truth about the bullying she was experiencing at school. The situation was 'diagnosed' during yet another visit to the doctor. Given her mother's obvious inability to cope with her own seemingly endless and largely unfounded anxieties, it is little wonder that Roxana had a negative outlook on life and was often beset by overwhelming anxieties of her own.

A need for appropriate support from teachers

This case study would suggest that before pupils like Roxana can play an active and consistent role in their own education they need to:

- be made aware of their anxieties;
- learn to put them in perspective and thus reduce their incidence;
- learn strategies which will help them to avoid or overcome anxiety.

For pupils silenced in the classroom by acute and often irrational anxieties, personal development involves learning new, more positive and secure ways of being. Where will they learn these if not at school? Attachment theory would suggest that there are benefits for anxious or insecure pupils in being able to rely on key members of staff to act as a 'secure base' from which they gradually learn increased independence. Where teachers are unable or unwilling to fulfil such a role, professional counselling staff may be needed to provide temporary support for anxious pupils like Roxana.

Case Study Two: Aberash: silenced by a clash of cultures

Aberash's case study also supports the theory that quiet withdrawn behaviour can be associated with anxious or insecure attachments with parents or significant others. Certainly, this case study would suggest that Aberash's acute withdrawal from the social and academic life of the classroom was due, in part, to early and prolonged separation from her mother. However, there is also evidence that Aberash's experience of conflicting values between her black family and her predominantly white school was an additional and major contributor to her quiet non-participatory behaviour.

Early childhood relationships with mother

Aberash lived with her mother and had little contact with her natural father. Aberash mentioned him briefly – 'I went to London with my Dad' – and suggested that at eleven, she was just 'getting to know Dad ... but it takes – it took a bit of time to get to know my Dad but it's alright'.

Aberash talks a lot more about her stepfather than her natural father. Her stepfather had moved into the family home when she was 11, and from the way Aberash described him he was full of fun and always teasing her. Nevertheless, Aberash experienced some difficulty in adapting to her new extended family.

Aberash's early childhood was spent with her mother who gave an extremely positive account of their early relationship. Aberash was a 'perfect baby' who didn't cry but was 'very responsive'. 'As a baby she was fun, very responsive. We spent a lot of time with each other in the early days and she was very responsive. Deep ... oh ... she didn't cry a lot so I thought she was a perfect baby.' However, whilst Aberash and her mother may have spent a lot of time together in the early months, economic necessity linked with a strong desire to better herself meant that Aberash's mother spent an increasing amount of time at work, leaving Aberash to be cared for by a series of childminders and relatives. Her mother creates a rosy image of an extended family. 'I know she had a good two to three years at nursery before she actually started school and it's a lot of things like she used to, we used to go to the park, spend time with different female members of the family.'

However, it is possible that Aberash does not have the same positive view of this extended family as her mother, 'because my mum's a bit boring most of the time, she sends me to my grandma's, but I like staying at home'.

Moreover, it became clear that Aberash linked her mother's return to work with her own loss of confidence: 'then she had to ... sometimes she had to go to work then I was a ... then when I had to go into the swimming baths again I was afraid to go in the water.' In addition to being cared for by members of the family, Aberash attended full-time nursery school from the age of two or three. Her transfer to infant school meant another change of routine in that the school insisted that she begin by attending on a half-day basis. This resulted in the need for a childminder to care for her before and after school, leaving her with little contact with her mother when she returned in the evening. Presumably such arrangements were further complicated if either Aberash or the childminder was ever ill.

Whilst Aberash's mother emphasized how much time she spent with her daughter during the first months of life, it would seem that from the age of two Aberash was cared for by a number of relatives, friends and teachers. Aberash's mother's reliance on others to care for her daughter continued throughout her childhood. Aberash explained how she preferred living with her grandma to moving to a new city with her mother. 'My mum's moving and I might be staying with grandma. Yeah, 'cos I'm not staying with me mum. Not bothered 'cos she's moving to another city, so I'm staying with my grandma not move. She asked me if I wanted to go and I said no.' Aberash's decision to stay with her grandmother is surprising since she had previously said how she preferred being at home with her mother. Moreover, it suggests a lack of attachment with her mother.

Early and prolonged separation from her mother and father could have influenced Aberash's behaviour in the classroom. Her inability or unwillingness to enter into relationships with teachers and peers could be related to her experience of not forming attachments with the scores of individuals who were entrusted with her care. Certainly, there is no doubt that, whatever the cause, Aberash was unable or unwilling to communicate with her teacher (see Chapter Two).

A conflict of cultures

Another cause of Aberash's quiet behaviour in school could be related to the conflict which her family sees between their black culture and that of the school. Aberash's mother is aware

117

of how these differences can affect an individual's behaviour and their perception of themselves.

> I mean I've been through it myself, you're two people, you're like the kind of person that you are at school that is told right 'You're the same as everybody else' and mix in and then you go home and there's a different, formal, sort of unwritten rule of education that's happening at home in terms of how you are and how your definitions are.

This 'separate existence' has its origins in the fact that neither teachers nor parents fully know, or respect, what goes on in the other aspects of a child's life. Thus pupils like Aberash are denied the opportunity to integrate the different aspects of their lives. Aberash's 'excluding' behaviour might well be connected with her need to be 'two people' which could impair her self-esteem and lead to 'a complete suppression of the spontaneous individual self' (Horney, 1939, p. 91). Certainly evidence collected during one-to-one interviews suggested that, even in these relatively secure situations, Aberash is hesitant to reveal anything of herself or her feelings.

What is not clear from Aberash's mother's comments about a 'separate existence' is the extent to which she felt that home and school should represent different ideas and values. However, it does seem as if Aberash had begun to make links between the different aspects of her life by seeing her school-friends at home. A crucial factor in this development could well be her mother's reaction to Aberash's new-found friends.

Aberash's seeming reluctance to mix with her peers in school may also stem from her view that racial tensions are sometimes exacerbated by attempts to integrate different races. She assumed that the teasing she suffered from members of her class were racial in origin.

> Probably because I'm black. Right, they're saying black words right and then they start using them against black people like in Nottingham when you have a row with a white person suddenly this black group comes round, they start giving you dirty looks. The black people start cussing the white people, it's not really

the white people 'cos it's you, the black people shouldn't be hanging round with them 'cos you know you're gonna get dirty looks from other black groups.

When asked if she was suggesting that black people should not mix with white people her reply was quick and decisive, 'Not if they're gonna use it against black people, start calling them names'. Interviews with Aberash and her mother revealed that both were extremely proud of their West Indian origin and culture. When it was suggested that only first names would be used during the interviews to ensure anonymity Aberash replied that her name was West Indian and therefore rare, if not unique, in Britain.

In her comments about music and television Aberash demonstrated her awareness of racial inequality in the media. ''Cos – like I see a lot of actresses every day on TV and they're nearly all white 'cept for Cosby show and other stuff in America.' However, rather than creating natural links with other West Indian children in the class, this fierce pride seemed to act as yet another source of conflict in what the mother saw as the Anglicization of their culture. For example, her mother admitted to being concerned when Aberash began to talk about the non-black musicians idealized by many of her peers: 'I've not just let it happen, and pretended "well it's no big deal" – it is a big deal.'

For Aberash's family this is more than a difference in taste between the generations. Her mother saw it as an Anglicization of her culture to be countered by 'giving Aberash as many black images as possible'. Yet, Aberash's interest in popular music could have been seen as a positive development of shared links with her peers. The possibility of differing interpretations provides further evidence of possible conflict between the perceptions of home and school. The need for schools to be aware of, and respond appropriately to, potential conflict between home and school is discussed at length in Chapter Eleven.

Case Study Three: Diana: silenced by her expectations of school

This case study differs from the two previous ones in that Diana's habitually quiet non-participatory behaviour does not appear to be related to anxious or insecure attachments in early parent–child relationships. Indeed, Diana appears to have secure attachment with both her father and younger sister. In this case study Diana's quiet behaviour has its origins in her inability to form relationships with her teacher and her firm belief that 'good pupils' are quiet and compliant and don't ask their teacher for help or support. Insofar as this view of pupils as passive recipients of knowledge is created and sustained by teachers in school, it is relatively easy to persuade pupils like Diana to play a more active role in their education. However, Diana's behaviour in school may be further constrained by her perceptions of herself as a working-class girl destined to fulfil the socially prescribed role of wife and mother.

Relationship with father

Diana and her younger sister Dawn lived with their father, an unemployed painter and decorator, in a mid-terrace council house. Both girls maintained contact with their mother who left the family home after an 'amiable' divorce some years previously. Diana's accounts of her family confirm that both her father and sister are key figures in her life. Her mother, who is hardly mentioned except in the context of the divorce, remains a shadowy figure.

Diana's father is clearly her primary attachment figure. Confirming the view that fathers can parent children, Diana explains how he fulfils the role of both mother and father for herself and her sister.

Diana: Mm – like like a mum and a dad. And he helps my sister as well. He copes well.

JC: How do you mean he copes well?

Diana: Like you'd think a one parent would struggle but he don't, like he takes things easy.

Diana seems convinced of her father's ability to cope with the demands of being a lone parent. There is a suggestion in Diana's comments that her relationship with her father had changed since her mother left home. When she is asked to name the most important person in her life she hesitates, 'Er – er – there's quite a couple really but I shouldn't – my dad helps me a lot now, now my mum's left and that lot.' In the context of this interview it seems likely that Diana was going to name her mother as the most important person in her life. Whilst Diana's relationship with her mother is hardly mentioned, there is no doubt about the deep affection and love which runs through every exchange between father and daughter.

In addition to carrying out domestic duties Diana's father also took an active interest in her school life. It was to her father that Diana turned when she had a problem: 'He's like a teacher, my dad, really when he's got the time'. Diana constantly referred to her father and frequently quoted his opinion on a wide range of issues. He offered her security, and his praise added to the positive image she had of herself. 'And my proudest moment were when – I think it were when I were reading to my dad I think it were, and I didn't really get mixed words wrong and he said "Oh good girl" and things like that and I were proud of myself.'

Diana's father clearly appreciated the value of praise in building self-confidence. Diana quotes several examples of his encouraging his daughters by praising their modest successes. This supportive role is one which Diana frequently adopts in school during small group activities.

However, whilst Diana's father clearly wanted her to be more successful at school than he was, there was a limit to his aspirations for his daughter. Through his comments he effectively squashed her ambition to be a doctor. He could not envisage her in such a role. To him she is 'not a go-getter'. He is surprised by, and even laughs at, her ambition. 'All she

121

wants to do, if ever I ask her what she wants to be she says a doctor [laughter] I hope she can be but I doubt it. Or a nurse you know – I'm surprised she said doctor, there's a lot of girls say "I want to be a nurse" and things like that.' It would be easier for him to accept his daughter in a stereotypical female role than as a 'trend setter'. How far this is a realistic appraisal of Diana's potential it is difficult to say. Nevertheless, as the subsequent section of this case study shows, Diana was already modifying her ambition in the light of other people's perceptions of her. She was, to some extent at least, constrained by her father's narrow perception of her. On a deeper level there seems to be a need for Diana to establish herself as a separate person without losing the attachment which gives her such a secure base from which to grow. One positive sign is that she seems able to recognize the need for separation in her close relationship with her sister.

Relationship with sister

Diana was, by her own admission, more than usually close to her younger sister Dawn. Diana was not sure how far their close relationship was a product of their parents' divorce and how far it was due to the fact that Dawn was small for her age and therefore appeared vulnerable.

> Yeah, I think we're closer than other brothers and sisters 'cos sometimes they've got their mums and dads but me and Dawn we've got each other really haven't we? ... but I think that if my mum still lived with us we'd still be close as well because she's smaller than her age and – don't know why – but I'm just close to her.

Diana was clearly protective towards Dawn. Her father went so far as to describe her as a 'little mother'. In assuming the role of surrogate mother, Diana is once again fulfilling a female stereotype in which she perceives herself in relation to others. One effect of the close relationship is that Diana was preoccupied by her sister's needs. When she was asked three seemingly unrelated questions – 'What makes you angry?',

'Have you ever done anything you were ashamed of?' and 'Is there anything that scares you?' – all three were answered with reference to Dawn. Diana was made angry by people picking on Dawn. She worried that things were happening to Dawn. She was ashamed that she once hit her sister 'hard'. It was almost as if Diana did not have a separate existence outside her relationships with others.

Her relationship with Dawn certainly took up a lot of Diana's time. It may not have been an exaggeration when Diana said 'If I go out she is always with me'. Moreover,

> As soon as she's out of my sight I get worried and I go looking for her, right. Yesterday I were at my friend's house, right, listening to a tape and she weren't in the bedroom and I went downstairs and I'm shouting her and everything and she were on the front playing ... She'd got me right worried and I said 'come upstairs with me Dawn because you get me worried when you are on your own'.

This is a relationship of mutual dependency. Dawn looked to Diana to help her solve practical problems, such as bullying at school. Diana needed to be sure of Dawn's physical proximity. Perhaps unconsciously Diana felt that she could lose Dawn in the same way that she lost her mother. Certainly Diana was afforded a certain status as the capable older sister.

To some extent Diana was aware that her relationship with her sister was one of dependency. She also anticipated that a time would come when her sister would want to be more independent. Indeed, Diana suggested that she was beginning to facilitate this process. When asked how she would feel as her sister grew older Diana answered this in terms of a growing independence.

> I know, that's what I'm thinking about like, she's got to stick up for herself in some ways and I'm, I'm just doing all t' sticking up for her. I've got to like tell her now she's got to do things herself, be a bit more independent 'cos I like do lots of things for her and er – I help her and things and I'm telling her to do things herself now she's getting older.

123

Diana seemed increasingly aware of the need for independence in relationships, especially in her relationship with her sister. She seemed less convinced of her need to establish her separate identity from her father.

Not surprisingly, although close, Diana's relationship with her sister was not without its tensions. 'But I think it's better to have a little sister, even though she does get spoilt more. Well she don't really get spoilt more it's just that sometimes I feel left out but I'm not.' Diana had obviously spent some time reflecting on her relationship with her sister. She was sensitive enough to believe that relationships are both complex and fluid. Perhaps she needed to be encouraged to look beyond the relationships with others and establish her own personality, needs and ambitions.

Having experienced good relationships at home during early childhood, Diana was prepared to seek similarly secure relationships at school. However, she was prevented from taking an active role in her own education by a poorly developed sense of independent autonomy and by a limited view of what education can offer.

Expectations of school
Diana was a conscientious pupil. This was highlighted by her comments about transferring to secondary school where she will 'try and pass all my tests, to make friends and to try harder'. Diana wanted to do well in school because she saw this as the only way to achieve her long-term aim to be a doctor. However, there is evidence to suggest that she had begun to modify her goal in the light of other people's expectations. Diana told a friend of her ambition: 'And she said, "Oh God, you can't be a doctor because you've got to be so clever to be a doctor". And I thought, well, if I pass all my exams and start studying I might be able to be a doctor.' Even whilst affirming her intent she begins to modify her aim: 'And if not a doctor, a vet, and if not a vet a police lady.' A year later Diana was hesitant about stating her ambition, 'I'm trying to study but I want to like – be a person what helps people.' I

can only speculate as to the influences which led to Diana's reassessment of her career choices. However, in her choice of career as in her daily life Diana fulfils the female stereotype in seeing herself in relation to others.

In one sense an ultimate career should not be the preoccupation of her primary school teachers. For example, the primary school curriculum should not be dominated by the constraints of a public examination system. However, and this is so fundamental that it should not need to be said, pupils should have the opportunity to develop to their full potential irrespective of their gender, race or class. Whilst recognizing the developments in the area of equal opportunities, I would suggest that the hidden curriculum still supports female passivity. As I have already said, watching Diana and her friends in the classroom I was struck by how little space, either real or metaphysical, they occupied in the classroom. Whilst their male peers moved freely around the room the girls stayed quietly in their places. Moreover, the girls' role as providers of equipment and services was largely unchallenged by either pupils or teachers.

Diana was encouraged to believe that her quiet compliant behaviour was appropriate for achieving academic success. However, in reality it is likely to be the active pupils who ask questions of the teacher and make the learning their own who are the ones more likely to succeed. Moreover, she believes that she is getting a good education, which she defines as 'like being teached the right things and things like that, and being good at skills'. Ignoring for the moment her narrow definition of education as the learning of skills, I believe that Diana is not as successful as she might be in three major respects. First, and most importantly, she fails to engage with her class teacher in the active pursuit of knowledge. This is due to her lack of self-confidence and her failure to recognize the importance of talking with her teachers. Second, she has no clear assessment of her own strengths and weaknesses nor guidance as to how she can improve. She has no clear short-term objectives to aim for. Finally, there is a mismatch between her experiential out-

125

of-school knowledge and the book-based learning valued in school.

Relationships with teachers

Diana had no difficulty in connecting talk with the formulation and expression of good ideas. To her, good talkers are 'people that come out with good ideas'. Moreover, she admitted that she had her fair share of good ideas at home. The reason why she was reluctant to share them at school was revealed when she described the behaviour of a fellow pupil. Diana began by describing Massaret but soon changed the 'she' to 'you' thus, perhaps unconsciously, including herself in the group of people who find it difficult to volunteer answers in class.

> She never even says owt, probably because she's too shy because sometimes they think of good things and think 'No, people might think it's daft' and you're worried about what other people're thinking but then say he asks someone else a question and they say the answer that you thought of, teacher says it's not daft, but you're always worried about what other people'll think rest of the time.

A lack of confidence and a fear of other people's scorn prevented Diana from answering the teacher's questions. Her frustration when she found that she had the right answer is clear. Thus opportunities for dialogue with the teacher are limited by her concern for what other people might say. If, as Diana suggests, some pupils are inhibited in this way, this calls into question the value of whole-class discussions, especially if such discussions constitute the major part of pupil–teacher dialogue.

More worrying still was Diana's assumption that she was somehow outside the group of those who were being taught. When asked if she talked to the teacher she said that she did. However, her account of such an exchange suggested how limited such a dialogue might be. 'When I am stuck he has to help me ... work and everything but most of the time he's like talking his self like doing things on the board and things so you can't really talk to him when he's trying to learn children.' 'Most of the time' Diana felt that she could not talk to the teacher because he was teaching the children. For her, teaching clearly involves a transmission of knowledge from teacher to pupils who act as passive recipients. There is no indication here that Diana, or indeed her teacher, regarded education as a collaborative search for knowledge through dialogue. Moreover, Diana excluded herself from the group of children being taught. It seems that there needs to be a change of attitude and practice before Diana, and pupils like her, can actively engage in the learning process. I believe that closer relationships between pupils and teachers are central to this development.

Read together, these case studies highlight several issues which are central to an understanding of the link between parent–child relationships and quiet withdrawn behaviour. They demonstrate how an understanding of parent–child relationships may provide insights into a child's behaviour in school and consequently the need for good relationships and dialogue between teachers and parents. However, these case studies also highlight the fact that, as parent–child relationships are complex, there is a need to ensure that psychological theories of attachment behaviour are not inappropriately applied. Anxious or inappropriate parent–child relationships are not the sole cause of quiet non-participatory behaviour in schools. Teachers have to be aware of, and take some responsibility for, the 'in-school factors' which contribute to quiet non-participatory behaviour. An account of teaching strategies which have proved successful in empowering quiet withdrawn pupils forms the basis of Part Three of this book.

Part Three
The Teachers

8 Encouraging quiet children to participate

In order to meet the individual needs of quiet pupils, I began by working with them in small groups withdrawn from the mainstream classroom. I hoped that this would help to create a secure and supportive environment in which they could learn and develop strategies for effective classroom talk without fear of teasing from more confident and vocal peers. I also hoped that working in small groups would be effective in boosting self-confidence within the small groups and ultimately encourage pupils to play a more active role once they return to whole-class situations. This chapter provides an account of my work with quiet children in small groups withdrawn from the mainstream classroom. The ways in which I then adapted my teaching strategies for use in a whole-class context are discussed in Chapter Nine.

Rationale for withdrawal

At the time of writing the educational climate was such that the decision to withdraw pupils from their mainstream classroom was tied up with a number of practical and ideological issues. I propose to discuss the possible objections to the withdrawal of pupils and outline the reasons why I value this particular approach when working with habitually quiet pupils.

Perhaps the most important objection to withdrawal is that it appears to run counter to current trends of integrating pupils with special educational needs into mainstream schools and classrooms. The integration versus withdrawal debate which has dominated special education over recent years assumes that equality of opportunity is synonymous with equality of access. However, whilst I favour the principle of the integration of pupils with special needs into mainstream schools, I would argue that quiet pupils are denied equality of opportunity because their behaviour prevents them from making the most of the educational opportunities presented to them. Moreover, as supported by the success of the reading recovery programme (Wade and Moore, 1993b), children can benefit tremendously from short intensive programmes designed to focus on their specific needs. In defence of my decision to withdraw pupils I would point out that the programme of withdrawal was short (one hour a week), temporary (for 12 weeks) and with a specific focus (developing oral skills).

However, despite my confidence in the possible benefits of short-term withdrawal, I was worried that the pupils might be stigmatized by my decision to include them in the small group activities. As the pupils were not being selected on academic ability I felt that this was less likely than might have been the case if the group had been focusing on specific learning difficulties such as basic literacy skills. Nevertheless, as a precaution, I did not explain to the pupils why they had been chosen beyond the fact that I was interested in working with them. If the issue of their quiet withdrawn behaviour or, as they called it, their shyness, was discussed, this was only after the subject was raised by the pupils themselves.

Interestingly, whilst the school I was working in did not resist on ideological grounds the idea of withdrawal of pupils with special educational needs, both the class teacher and the headteacher had their own reasons for favouring whole-class teaching. These reasons are discussed at length because they may be indicative of attitudes in the teaching profession as a whole.

The teacher's objection was that where whole-class teaching is the norm, withdrawing pupils on a regular basis disrupts teaching schedules. He felt that, whilst pupils benefit from withdrawal programmes, these benefits have to be weighed against the fact that pupils miss other lessons or activities. Pupils, especially the less able, may have difficulty in making up for lost time or in picking up the threads of ongoing topic work. Obviously these effects are likely to be minimized where the classes are organized as small group activities or an integrated day. The headteacher's resistance to my working exclusively with withdrawal groups stemmed from a belief that such work was not regarded, either by herself or by the profession as a whole, as real teaching. For example, during a lunch-time conversation she asked me how my work was developing. She was particularly interested in how it contributed to my professional development. I talked at length about the benefits, to both pupil and teacher, of being able to withdraw pupils to work in small groups. However, she was particularly interested in my decision to develop this work in a whole-class situation. 'Ah', she said, 'so that is the professional development.' The implication was that, whilst withdrawal groups were interesting, 'real teaching' involved working with whole classes.

In addition, both the teacher and headteacher were aware of practical considerations which have to be overcome in order to provide opportunities for small group withdrawal. Providing additional staff and teaching space is likely to be extremely difficult in schools faced with falling budgets, staff reductions and increasing class sizes. Where additional resources are impossible we need to think in terms of redistributing existing provision. Existing withdrawal programmes which focus on basic literacy could be adopted to focus occasionally on the needs of habitually quiet pupils. This could be justified in terms of the National Curriculum Orders for English in which Speaking and Listening are given the same status as Reading and Writing. Support staff and classroom assistants currently employed within the classroom could be redirected to spend some time working specifically with quiet pupils. Where withdrawal is impossible small-group activities focusing on developing skills in oracy could be established in classrooms, although there children have neither privacy nor

133

the continued support of the teacher. Whilst acknowledging the practical and ideological difficulties which schools face, there are three reasons why I would still advocate short programmes of withdrawal for habitually quiet pupils.

First, there is a need to devise and implement teaching strategies which are specifically geared to meeting the needs of habitually quiet pupils. Working in withdrawal groups which exclude loud, potentially aggressive pupils seems an ideal way to assess and meet those needs. Second, there is a need to provide a secure environment in which the pupils do not have to compete with their more vocal peers. Small-group work provides a useful non-competitive environment for pupils to practise and develop their oral skills. Third, participating in small group discussions might, of itself, encourage pupils to contribute more freely than they would be willing and able to do in a whole-class discussion. If this were the case it would confirm a link between inappropriate teaching strategies and quiet withdrawn behaviour in schools.

Withdrawal groups provide pupils with an opportunity to work with other quiet pupils and develop skills which they can practise in relative security before trying them out in a whole-class context. As a consequence, whilst I understand current reservations about withdrawing pupils with special educational needs, I would maintain that such work can have tremendous benefits for the pupils. The criteria for appropriate withdrawal should be that the withdrawal be short, temporary and focused. I believe that my withdrawal of the quiet pupils from their mainstream classroom met all three criteria as well as my aims in setting up the programme.

Aims of the withdrawal programme

The overall aim of the withdrawal programme was to empower habitually quiet pupils to take an active role in their education. Embodied in this aim were specific teaching and learning objectives which helped to identify appropriate teaching strategies and also criteria by which I could determine the relative success of the programme. Where the objectives were made explicit to the pupils they provided a basis for pupil self-assessment.

I began my work with four distinct but related objectives.

First, I wanted the pupils to appreciate the importance of talk in learning. By establishing a series of lessons devoted to the development of communication skills I wanted pupils to have experience of both learning about talk and learning through talk.

Second, I wanted the pupils to participate in, and contribute to, small-group discussions with their peers. In order for pupils to be willing and able to contribute in this way I aimed to create a learning situation which offered an appropriate balance of security and challenge. To achieve this, I intended to consider both the teaching approaches used and the content of the discussions.

Third, I wanted the pupils to make the learning their own. By encouraging them to ask questions and introduce their own agendas I wanted pupils to 'name their world'. Supporting child-centred learning of this kind has clear implications for the role of the teacher who is required to act as facilitator.

Finally, as quiet withdrawn behaviour is often related to poor self-esteem, my fourth objective was to encourage pupils to feel good about themselves. I hoped that the pupils would gain self-confidence both from their experience of success in the small-group discussions and from being valued by their peers.

In addition to meeting these aims, my work with quiet withdrawn pupils also met several of the objectives set out in the National Curriculum Orders for Speaking and Listening, Key Stage 2. For example, pupils should be given opportunities to talk for a range of purposes, including:

- exploring, developing and explaining ideas;
- sharing ideas, insights and opinions;
- reading aloud, telling and enacting stories and poems;
- reporting and describing events and observations;
- presenting to audiences, live and on tape.

135

In addition, 'Pupils should be given opportunities to participate in a wide range of drama activities, including improvisation, role-play, and the writing and performance of scripted drama' (DFE, 1995, p. 11). These aims formed the basis of the withdrawal programme.

The withdrawal programme

The focus on talk

In establishing the importance of talk for learning, I wanted pupils to experience and appreciate the ways in which they could learn, and subsequently demonstrate their learning, through the medium of the spoken word. Consequently, within the withdrawal group programme talk was the medium for learning. In the context of these activities, effective talk was seen as an end in itself. Thus, in contrast to lessons I had observed in the mainstream classroom, talk was the primary focus of the activity and not a precursor to the 'real' or main task of writing. Given the transitory nature of discussions, I found tape-recorders invaluable. Tape-recordings provided me with an opportunity to reflect on group discussions and analyse the contributions made by individual pupils. Whilst it was not part of my brief, such techniques would also be invaluable for assessing pupil progress within the Attainment Targets of the National Curriculum. In addition to using the tapes for teacher assessment I also used excerpts of successful discussions as teaching aids to give pupils an opportunity to discuss the nature of their talk. Peer review and self-assessment of talk became a brief but important feature of most withdrawal sessions and led to the development of the self-assessment sheets which I later used with the whole class (see Chapter Nine for further information).

Talk was the medium for learning and also, especially in the early sessions, the subject of our discussion. Fear of talking in front of groups of relative strangers was one of the few things which these pupils had in common. Therefore, workshop activities which focused on those fears seemed to be a useful way of introducing the subject of talk and finding common ground within the group. Naturally, it was important to find non-threatening ways to introduce the topics and I found 'diamond-ranking' exercises were a particularly effective way to initiate discussion. In a diamond-ranking activity each pupil was given nine pieces of card on each of which was written a situation in which they might talk to a specific group of people, for example, 'in front of the whole school', 'with friends' or 'at home with my family'. The task was to rank these situations in order of difficulty so that those in which the pupils found talking relatively easy would go at the top with the more difficult ones at the bottom. The purpose of the diamond shape (1, 2, 3, 2, 1,) was that the easiest and most difficult situations were clearly identified.

Once the pupils had ranked the situations the next task was for each pupil to share their answers with the rest of the group. This they did by reading out the statements which they had at the top and bottom of their personal diamond. At this point I stressed the importance of the pupils expressing their own point of view and that, as there were no right and wrong answers, we were not aiming to reach a consensus decision. As each pupil read out their two statements the rest of the group were encouraged to ask appropriate questions to find out more about how the individual felt in those situations. My role was to encourage the pupils to participate in the activity. I wanted them to take their turn in reading out their chosen statements and be prepared to ask questions of the other pupils. Here, as elsewhere, I tried hard not to direct the discussion nor to impose my own agenda beyond setting the initial task.

By structuring the discussion in this way I hoped to provide an environment in which all the pupils would be able to express an opinion about their experience of talking in a variety of situations. Indeed, this proved to be the case. Whilst some pupils were more reluctant than others, all the pupils were able to complete the task. In addition, all the pupils were able to expand on their original statements and answer the questions posed by their peers. Moreover, although some were more vocal than others, all the pupils took turns in asking questions and seeking additional information.

In addition to providing a tightly structured, and therefore relatively secure, opportunity for discussion to develop, this activity also highlighted the fact that the group shared similar experiences and concerns. In my opinion this brought the group together and I believe that incidents like this may well have been the foundation of many of the friendships which developed between the pupils. Certainly, as my work developed, friendships grew between pupils who had previously seemed to be social isolates in the classroom.

One of the features of quiet pupils' talk in school is that, whilst they may respond to questions from others, they are unlikely to initiate conversations. Consequently, it was important to encourage pupils to ask questions as a way of initiating or sustaining conversations. During the withdrawal programme pupils were asked to comment on the relative effectiveness of open and closed questions. They also considered the benefits of 'playing devil's advocate' and considering alternative points of view as a way of generating discussion. In addition, pupils were encouraged to listen attentively to others in order to be able to develop discussion. During the second half of the withdrawal programme I also used excerpts from *The Trouble with Donovan Croft* by Bernard Ashley (1977) to develop the discussion about the emotional aspects of speech and the possible relationship between self-image and talk.

An appropriate balance of security and challenge

Since quiet pupils are often anxious about speaking in front of others, I attempted to provide an appropriate level of security by setting tasks which were both structured and open-ended. Pupils were given a lot of scope to respond in their own way within a relatively tight structure. Given the pupils' embarrassment at being chosen to speak in class, I felt that knowing when it was their turn to speak and what was expected of them was likely to reduce their anxiety. Consequently, in the withdrawal groups, pupils always knew when they would be asked to respond and basically what form their contribution should take.

In introducing the idea of small-group discussions the initial problem was that the pupils involved were not familiar with this kind of approach. Although in their mainstream classroom the majority of the pupils sat together in groups, they tended to work individually. In this context co-operative tasks were rare. Moreover, talk in the mainstream classroom was strictly controlled by the class teacher. In one-to-one interviews, several of the pupils expressed a view that talking in class was naughty and not encouraged by the teacher. Indeed, during my observation of the class, pupils were sometimes allowed to sit with their friends on the understanding that they would not talk to each other. However, invariably this instruction was neither meant nor applied literally. So long as pupil conversations were reasonably quiet and task-related, pupils were unlikely be chastised for talking.

Within the withdrawal group feelings of security were enhanced by the fact that I remained present during all of the early sessions. Although I was anxious to allow the pupils' discussions to develop naturally and with minimum intervention from me, nevertheless, my role of chair ensured that the discussions were sustained. When I began a process of gradual withdrawal from the discussions I initially experienced some difficulty in persuading pupils to talk to each other rather than using me as an intermediary. Invariably when pupils wanted to speak they began by trying to attract my attention. When it was their turn to speak they would direct their comments at me rather than towards their peers. Gradually however, the pupils realized that what I wanted was for them to talk to each other and they began to take a more active role in the discussions. Increasingly the pupils began to introduce their own topics which they subsequently discussed among themselves without my intervention. When this happened I felt that the quality of the communication changed and became more naturalistic with questions being asked as part of a genuine attempt to understand another person's point of view. As the pupils became more able and willing to talk with each other I began to withdraw from the group discussions and I introduced independent group activities in which the pupils took increasing responsibility for their work. I felt that it was important for me to begin the withdrawal sessions with me acting as chair and providing a role model during teacher-led discussions. However, if the pupils were to be successful in small-group discussions which took place in the mainstream classroom, it was important for them to be able to work with their peers independently of their teacher. Consequently, independent group work was a natural progression.

Despite the fact that the pupils had gone some way towards overcoming their reluctance to join in with teacher-led discussions, the suggestion that they should participate in independent peer discussions immediately raised further problems. Pupils expressed initial resistance to the idea of working with their peers in this way. Even in the context of the withdrawal group where there was little fear of rejection, some of the pupils found it difficult to find a partner to work with. Whilst these aspects of pupil behaviour created problems for me in trying to organize the activities, it also validated my claim that quiet pupils should be considered as having special educational needs. Before looking at the pupils' response to the withdrawal programme it is important to consider how I began to address the pupils' inability or unwillingness to work with their peers.

Working with peers
Given that many of the pupils highlighted by the study had difficulty in forming and sustaining relationships, I decided that much of this early work would focus on the subject of relationships, primarily peer group relationships. Using excerpts from books like *The Trouble with Donovan Croft*, the pupils were encouraged to discuss aspects of relationships as portrayed by others. I also encouraged the pupils to participate in role-play

exercises in which they 'became' the different characters and therefore experienced 'first hand' something of how the characters might have felt. In these, as in all activities, I encouraged pupils to personalize the discussion by relating it to their own experiences. I also tried to encourage the pupils to set their own agenda by allowing discussions or activities to be shaped by their own concerns. For example, when Diana expressed concern about what she saw as blatant racism in *The Trouble with Donovan Croft*, I felt that it was appropriate to set aside the proposed agenda in order to discuss the issue. Similarly, Vicky's definition of friendship became the foundation for subsequent discussion. Both these examples are discussed below.

Pupil response to the withdrawal programme

Initial difficulties

As mentioned earlier, the suggestion that pupils should work in pairs or small groups met with some reluctance. At first Aberash refused, saying that she worked better alone. When I pointed out that talking was a shared activity she grudgingly agreed to take part. Roxana was similarly reluctant to find a partner among the group she was working with. On numerous occasions she suggested that she would work better with a pupil not included in the small group activities. As she named a different pupil on each occasion it seemed likely that this was a strategy designed to delay the process of having to find a partner. By contrast other pupils did not seem to have difficulty in finding a partner. Left to their own devices, Diana, Mandy and Justina always chose to sit and work together. Anxious that they should occasionally increase their circle of friends, I sometimes encouraged, or directed, them to work with other people.

When left to work without my supervision pupils occasionally complained that their discussion had been unfairly dominated by particular pupils. For example, on one occasion

141

Justina expressed the view that the previous discussion had been dominated by Aberash. Although all the pupils had talked for similar amounts of time, Justina felt that the group had been compelled to accept Aberash's point of view throughout. The ways in which individuals gain, maintain and exhibit authority over others was a recurring theme throughout. A related theme, and one which fascinated pupils, was the ways in which individuals could assert themselves without causing open conflict.

On other occasions pupils were openly intolerant of their peers. For example, in the transcript which follows Aberash and Justina appeared anxious that Vicky should play her part in the discussion. They pestered her unmercifully.

Aberash: Friends make you feel special
Justina: I think it should go sometimes
Aberash: Yeah, sometimes ... it's not always
Justina: What do you think Vicky? ... Vicky come into the discussion then ... What do you think?
Aberash: Er ...
Justina: Come on Vicky please
Aberash: Come on
Justina: If you don't ...
Aberash: Count to ... count to ... count to ten 'cos that's the only way you can do it ... you've got to ... you can't ... Miss will get mad with you you know. If you don't ... if you don't talk
Justina: Come on Vicky
Vicky: I don't know
Justina: Well think then we haven't got all day.

Needless to say, Vicky's response to this onslaught was to say very little indeed. Subsequent discussion suggests that whilst both Aberash and Justina realized the futile and potentially cruel nature of their behaviour they could not think of more positive ways of trying to encourage Vicky to participate. Fortunately, such incidents were rare. As the withdrawal programme progressed and pupils became used to working with their peers they became even fewer, and pupils could be observed using more supportive strategies. Moreover, the withdrawal programme proved extremely successful in encouraging the quiet pupils to participate in small-group discussions. This success is demonstrated in the following brief case studies.

Roxana practises telling her story

Right from the beginning Roxana was prepared to join in with small group discussions. However, in the early sessions her mannerisms and tone of voice suggested that she found the experience more difficult than she was prepared to admit. During these sessions Roxana's obvious anxiety meant that she often spoke very loudly and in a tone which suggested a presentation rather than a natural conversation. Moreover, when she became conscious of how she sounded she became even more self-conscious, putting her hand over her mouth and giggling. At times like this I encouraged her to pause for a moment and collect her thoughts. However, rather than relaxing into a more natural conversational tone she would simply repeat the same 'presentation'. Within the withdrawal group the other pupils and I were able to be far more supportive than would have been possible during whole-class discussions. Perhaps because they empathized with her difficulties, the other pupils responded positively to the content of what Roxana had to say and made no reference to her style of presentation. Moreover, they were prepared to tolerate long pauses and wait for her to compose herself after bouts of giggling.

As the sessions continued Roxana appeared increasingly more relaxed. Yet she continued to benefit from an opportunity to rehearse what she wanted to say. For example, during a whole-class lesson Roxana gave her partner an interesting but rather garbled account of an incident which had happened to a neighbour. Later in the same lesson Roxana told her story again to a slightly different audience. On the second occasion she seemed better able to organize her thoughts and the second account was much clearer. On this occasion Roxana used the opportunity to practise telling her story to great effect (for further discussion of this incident see Chapter Nine). That pupils may need time to gather and arrange their thoughts has implications for the way talk is organized in the classroom. Whilst rehearsing a contribution to a discussion should not be either compulsory or too tightly structured, pupils may, on occasion, benefit from being able to tell their story in different ways and for different audiences. My experience suggests that self-conscious pupils like Roxana benefit from being able to control the pace of talk-related activities in order to meet their individual and specific needs.

Vicky sets the agenda

One of the greatest and most pleasing aspects of this work was in observing Vicky play a full role in the discussions. This pupil, who exhibited extreme withdrawal in the classroom, found her voice during small-group sessions in which I was present and acting as chair. One particular session began with the pupils taking part in role-play situations when they acted out a number of scenes in which characters tried, with varying degrees of success, to make friends with their peers. In order to emphasize positive experiences, during the subsequent discussion pupils were asked to think of situations in which they had experienced acts of friendship. Without hesitation Vicky cited the example of how nurses had recently shown friendship to her sick grandfather. This unexpected contribution prompted interesting discussion of the nature of friendship and the different forms it might take. The outcome was far more interesting than the mere account of incidents in school which I had anticipated.

Obviously, a discussion of the factors which contributed to Vicky's feeling able and willing to contribute in this way is, by definition, pure speculation. However, I can suggest two possible reasons why she spoke out. It could be that participation in role-play encouraged her to imagine situations beyond the 'here and now' reality of the classroom. If this is the case then participation in the role-play which encouraged pupils to imagine alternative scenarios may have helped Vicky to make the link between friendship as experienced in the role-play and her grandfather's situation. She was attempting to 'name her world' by making links between different aspects of her life. However, an alternative interpretation could be that Vicky had predicted that the discussion was likely to centre on school-based relationships and had chosen to direct the discussion in a different way. As she did not appear to have a close friend in the school she could have wanted to avoid what might have been an uncomfortable, if not painful, discussion. If this is the case then her contribution could be seen as an attempt to exert some control over her environment. This interpretation would support my view that her frequent refusal to speak was an indication of a need or desire for control. Certainly in this situation she had her wish. The discussion became a consideration of examples of friendship in the wider community with other pupils citing examples of acts of friendship shown by people outside school.

Whatever it was that prompted Vicky to talk about her grandfather in the way she did, I felt that it was important for her to have the experience of 'naming her world' in her own terms. This example demonstrates the value of small-group discussions in empowering quiet pupils. It is possible that, had the discussion taken place in a whole-class situation, Vicky would have simply kept quiet, assuming, perhaps rightly, that it was unlikely she would be asked to participate. Nevertheless, in retrospect I wish that I had been more aware of the different possible interpretations of her action during the actual discussion. Had this been the case I might have been able to discuss it with Vicky and thus gain insights into her extreme withdrawal which bordered on 'elective mutism'.

Diana talks about her own experience
Diana was so confident in the small-group situation that she frequently drew analogies between the issues raised during discussions and her own lived experiences. For example, in

Session 8 the focus was on Donovan's experience of fostering. Diana immediately related this to her friend's experiences in a similar situation.

> I know a girl called Kelly once and she were adopted. And I don't think it were fair 'cos she had to go to different houses. And when she was in this house that I knew her in the parents weren't treating her right, well foster parents they weren't treating her right ... and her sister, well her foster sister, she were getting more attention than Kelly and when Kelly just got a bit of attention Joanne, her foster sister, got all jealous and they had to get rid of Kelly she had to go to a different house ... And Kelly said that she felt all miserable and horrible and that she wanted to find her parents again.

It is significant that in telling her story Diana was prepared to go beyond the actual facts of the case. She talked about how being rejected by yet another foster family made her friend feel miserable and long for a family of her own. Diana also expresses her own point of view. She does this directly with phrases such as 'I don't think it were fair', and also in her implied criticism of Joanne's jealousy when Kelly 'got just a bit of attention'. I felt that this expression of personal experience was useful to the whole group in that the other pupils could learn from Diana's experience in a way which would enhance their reading of the text. Moreover, Diana was providing an excellent role model for her peers.

It was later in the same session that Diana suggested that it was inappropriate for Donovan's foster family to consider that Donovan's being black might be a problem for a white family. Turning to her West Indian friend for support, Diana stated that black and white people were the same and should be treated as such. At the time I was aware that as these two incidents followed immediately one after the other it was possible that gaining confidence during the story-telling might have encouraged Diana to take the risk of accusing the teacher of using racist material. I was pleased that, rather than being defensive, which would have effectively ended the discussion, I was confident enough to lead a discussion on the relative merits of the book. Interestingly, the two West Indian pupils present had little to say on the subject of racism during this original discussion. However, they were prepared to express their feelings in subsequent one-to-one discussions. Here, as on numerous other occasions, I appreciated the benefits of supporting my teaching with an opportunity to have one-to-one conversations with pupils. This luxury is not ordinarily available to class teachers but my experience would suggest that it should be.

In conclusion, the 12-week withdrawal programme proved to be effective in empowering quiet pupils to participate in small-group discussions. The style and content of these discussions seemed to go some way to meeting the pupils' specific educational needs. However, two questions remained unanswered. First, to what extent was it possible to develop co-operative small-group activities in a whole-class context? Secondly, given an appropriate and relatively secure environment, would the quiet pupils be able to transfer their new-found skills and confidence to work with their more vocal and volatile peers? Through an account of my work with the quiet pupils in their mainstream classroom the following chapter provides an answer to those questions.

9 Teaching strategies for the whole class

The previous chapter examined the ways in which I met the needs of quiet children in the relatively secure environment of a withdrawal group. This chapter extends and develops this work by describing ways in which the needs of quiet pupils can be met through small-group activities organized in a whole-class context. Underpinning this chapter is the notion that increasing quiet pupils' participation involves changing the behaviour of all pupils. Quiet pupils have to be encouraged to be more assertive and find their voice in the classroom. At the same time more vocal pupils have to be persuaded to talk less and be a suitably appreciative audience for quiet pupils.

> For example, where pupils have difficulties in peer relationships which interfere with their learning, it is important not only to help them as individuals to develop their confidence and social skills, but also to work with the class as a whole in order to ensure that they do not become the subject of teasing, ridicule or rejection.
> (Beveridge, 1993, p. 96)

As quiet pupils are aware of the ways in which they are disadvantaged by their habitually quiet behaviour, they have a lot to gain from a change in the group dynamics of the classroom. Consequently it is far easier to encourage them to talk than it is to persuade their more vocal peers to occasionally refrain from talking. Here it is possible to draw analogies between working with quiet pupils and working with the victims of bullying. In both cases the 'victims' welcome a change in behaviour whilst the dominant groups perceive a

148

change of behaviour as synonymous with a loss of power. In order to be successful I would have to devise and implement teaching strategies which would allow all pupils to have a voice in the classroom. My work was made particularly difficult as the class in question had little experience in peer collaboration. In addition the particular class I was working with contained a small number of extremely disruptive and potentially violent individuals. I was consoled by the knowledge that strategies which succeeded in this environment were likely to work in most classroom contexts.

As the previous chapter identified, small-group activities had already proved successful in empowering quiet pupils. Such groups:

- increase the amount of pupil talk;
- provide a relatively secure environment for pupils to explore their ideas and express themselves through talk;
- give the pupils some degree of autonomy over their learning;
- give the teacher an opportunity to stand back and reflect on the nature and quality of interactions between pupils.

The obvious next step was to devise ways of developing small-group activities with the whole class. In doing so I had to overcome a number of practical difficulties.

First, underlying all small-group collaboration is the issue of attitudes to talk in school. Despite the efforts of teachers inspired by initiatives like the National Oracy Project, many pupils continue to undervalue the importance of talk and regard it as a mere precursor to the 'real work' of writing. This belief is strengthened by the fact that, whilst teachers spend a great deal of time marking, correcting and grading pupils' writing, classroom talk is, by definition, transient and does not receive the same level of attention. Secondly, the complexity of peer relationships in school means that organizing classes into small groups can be problematic. Whilst popular children can choose from a number of potential partners other children are not so fortunate. When asked to find a partner some pupils are likely to hang back and refuse to participate, and others may be openly rejected by their peers. Small-group interactions are dependent on positive relationships between the participants, and teachers have to find ways of organizing their classes which make all pupils feel wanted and valued. The third problem is associated with the difficulties which pupils can experience in sustaining collaborative small-group activities, especially if they lack the social skills to work unsupervized. Discussions may break down, or may be dominated by more vocal individuals. Small-group activities also break down when pupils fail to resolve differences of opinion.

Having anticipated these and other potential difficulties, my aim was to create an intellectually stimulating and challenging programme to be delivered in a supportive and secure environment. I was aiming to meet both the demands of the National Curriculum Orders for English (DFE, 1995) and attain the characteristics of successful teaching as identified by Mortimore *et al.* (1988) and summarized in *School Effectiveness: Research, Policy and Practice* by Reynolds and Cuttance (1992). For Mortimore, the term 'effective' related to high performance in academic areas such as reading and writing and in non-academic areas, for example low truancy levels. However, I believe that the same principles apply to the teaching of oracy skills. From the summary prepared by Reynolds and Cuttance, I have identified a number of characteristics which have direct relevance to the teaching of oracy skills to classes of children which contain quiet and withdrawn pupils. These include:

- Consistency among teachers. Continuity of staffing had a positive effect but pupils also performed better when the approach to teaching was consistent.
- A structured day. Children performed better when their school day was structured in some way. In effective schools, pupils' work was organized by the teacher, who ensured there was plenty for them to do yet allowed them some freedom within the structure.
- Intellectually challenging teaching. Not surprisingly, pupil progress was greater where teachers were stimulating and enthusiastic. The incidence of 'higher order' questions and statements was seen to

be vital – that is, where teachers frequently made children use powers of problem solving.

- A work-centred environment. This was characterized by a high level of pupils' industry, with children enjoying their work and being eager to start new tasks.

In my work with quiet pupils in a mainstream classroom I aimed to be consistent and create a work-centred environment which was intellectually challenging and which at the same time offered the pupils an appropriate balance of structure and freedom.

Teaching strategies

As with the withdrawal group I began by making talk the main focus of the lessons. Talk was the medium for learning and was seen as an end in itself rather than as a precursor for writing. Consequently the only writing done during these lessons was note taking as an *aide-mémoire* for subsequent discussion or as part of a feedback presentation. Systematic recording, analysis and assessment of talk seemed to be sufficient to convince the pupils of the value of what they were doing. Reference to the National Curriculum, which gives speaking and listening equal status with reading and writing, added weight, in the staffroom as well as the classroom, to my assertion that talk was important.

In focusing on talk the pupils covered a wide range of issues which included Myself, Families, Friends, Becoming Independent and Experiencing Change. I drew on a range of stimuli to generate talk including: poetry, short stories, personal anecdotes, newspaper articles and packs of professionally produced pictures. These pictures were particularly effective in generating discussion on 'the nature of the family', 'breaking down gender stereotypes' and 'the nature of disability'. I also introduced the class to role-play activities which became extremely popular. This work took place in the context of sessions specifically designed to generate oracy skills. However, the materials used would indicate that a similar programme could be used as an integral part of an English programme; similarly, the nature of the subjects covered suggests that this work would lend itself to personal health and social education courses.

Producing a secure but challenging environment

Once I had decided to base my teaching on small-group activities, the first task was to overcome the feelings of anxiety and rejection which many pupils experience when they are required to work with their peers. I decided that, whilst there were merits to grouping pupils according to ability, the small-group activities would be based on friendship groups as chosen by the pupils themselves. As the quiet pupils had low self-esteem and/or difficulty in forming relationships, I believed that self-selected friendship groups would provide them with an appropriate source of security. In addition, having the same partner for a predetermined period removed the potentially traumatic uncertainties of having to find a partner at the start of every lesson. The subsequent success of the project began with the amazingly simple concept of talk partners and I feel that it is appropriate to begin by describing the process by which these were established.

Talk partners

I began with the assumption that, whilst some pupils would deny it, fear of rejection by one's peers is a common, if not universal, human experience. Consequently, I began the process of establishing talk partners by appealing unashamedly to the pupils' finer feelings by asking them to imagine how they would feel if they were excluded by their peers. I told the class a personal and, I felt, quite moving story about a girl I had known at school who was teased unmercifully by her peers. I admitted the ambivalence that I had felt in knowing the teasing was unfair but not having the courage to stand up to her tormentors. I also told how guilty and ashamed I had felt when she died prematurely a little after her seventeenth birthday. After this personal reflection I read the poem 'Tich Miller' by Wendy Cope and asked the pupils to reflect on situations in which they had witnessed acts of cruelty to others. In order to lighten the mood I then read the humorous poem 'Picking Teams' by Allen Ahlberg. Once again pupils were encouraged to identify links between the poem and their own lived experiences.

After this introduction I asked the pupils to nominate anonymously, by writing the names on a piece of paper, three pupils they felt they could work with for half a term. I stressed that as a class it was our responsibility to ensure that no one was left out of the process and that everyone had a 'talk partner'. I said that once I had collected in the pieces of paper I would organize the class into groups of two or three. Once these groups were established they would remain in place for half a term when, in order to take into account changes in relationships, the process would be repeated. Interestingly, despite my fears that some pupils might be social isolates, all the pupils in the class had at least one talk partner. Thus the groups were genuinely self-selecting and needed no adjustment from me. Nevertheless, I welcomed the anonymity of this process which ensured that no pupil faced the indignity of being left out or rejected by their peers. Interestingly, all the quiet pupils picked partners they had worked with as part of the withdrawal programme and it seemed that the relationships initiated in the withdrawal groups appeared to form the basis of subsequent friendships. The fact that the pupils, some of whom had previously behaved like social isolates, had a group of potential partners also helped to justify their involvement in the withdrawal groups.

Having predetermined, self-selected talk partners helped to overcome many of the practical difficulties I had previously experienced in trying to organize pupils into groups. All the pupils began each of the lessons knowing that they had a partner and that they would not be teased, left out or rejected. In this way pupils like Aberash, who had previously shown reticence to the idea of working with her peers, accepted the idea of small-group work.

153

I am convinced that having regular 'talk partners' offered quiet pupils with emotional and behavioural difficulties a much-needed degree of security which they would not necessarily experience if groups were organized in other ways. This was borne out by observations of the difficulties which pupils appear to experience when they are asked to work with, or perform in front of, a randomly chosen group of peers. For example, when I tried a strategy known as 'jigsawing', in which individuals leave their 'home group' to gather information from other groups, some pupils either refused to participate or became very distressed. Thus, whilst a variety of groupings may be appropriate for confident pupils familiar with small-group work, I felt that some pupils, especially those who were quiet and withdrawn, needed the security of working with chosen friends. Similarly, predetermined talk partners deprived the more vocal pupils of the opportunity to tease or bully their less confident peers.

In order to allow the pupils the opportunity to work with a larger variety of people I occasionally put several groups of 'talk partners' together. I explained that I would expect everyone to be able to cope with this because they always had the support of their chosen partner. Most of the time this worked very well and pupils adapted easily to the idea of plenary sessions in which they would 'report back' to a larger group of pupils. On the few occasions that I noticed pupils being marginalized or excluded I reminded everyone of the need to include everyone in their activity. When it seemed appropriate I talked with the class about verbal and physical strategies which were likely to include or exclude others. Reminding pupils of what I would accept as appropriate behaviour was usually sufficient to create a marked, if occasionally temporary, improvement in their behaviour.

In an attempt to make pupils aware of their behaviour and its possible effect on others, I regularly used audio- and video-recordings to illustrate examples of 'effective talk' and provided the pupils with an opportunity to analyse what had contributed to a particular group's success. As with the withdrawal programme, using excerpts of talk to illustrate positive aspects of group interactions was effective both in identifying the important aspects of interaction and in enhancing the self-esteem of the participants.

Whilst recorded talk was regularly used to highlight positive aspects of talk, on one occasion I felt compelled to use a video-tape to draw attention to negative behaviour. During the video-taping of one session in which I attempted to use the 'jigsawing' technique a number of boys deliberately shunned an Asian girl as she approached the table where the group were to be working. By moving their chairs and turning their backs, the group effectively isolated her and left her in no doubt that she was not welcome. Not surprisingly, subsequent attempts by other girls to involve the isolated pupil in the discussion failed. Appalled by the incident, my first instinct was to challenge the boys involved with what I saw as their inexcusable behaviour. The class teacher, however, suggested that I was naïve to expect the boys to work with girls and that a viewing of the video would only inflame the situation. In order that this incident should not go unchallenged, the teacher and I reached a compromise in which I showed the video to a group of children (including the quiet withdrawn pupils) who we knew would be sympathetic to the plight of isolated or rejected children. I am pleased to say that the viewing of the video led to a number of pupils 'adopting' this particular girl and ensuring that she had a fair opportunity to participate in their group work. I felt that showing the video had led to a marked improvement in the way in which this particular girl was treated by some of her peers. However, dealing with it in this way did little to tackle the blatant racism and sexism inherent in both the pupils' behaviour and the teacher's comments about it. How can we expect pupils to work in collaborative and egalitarian ways if we do not treat all pupils as equals?

The experience of using the 'jigsaw' technique convinced me that this particular class was not ready to work with relative strangers and we went back to using 'talk partners'. In order

155

to add to the feelings of security the lessons followed a similar, and therefore highly predictable, pattern.

The lessons

Especially during the first term, the lessons began with the whole class sitting in a large circle and participating in circle games or activities. The emphasis during this 'circle time' was for each pupil to have the opportunity to speak whilst the remainder of the pupils exhibited respectful silence. An opportunity for all pupils to speak at the beginning of the lesson is important, particularly for less confident pupils who are likely to find that their anxiety increases the longer it takes for them to 'break the ice'. In addition, I attempted to make participation in circle-time activities as stress-free as possible. For most games or activities the contribution expected from each pupil was short and followed a predetermined pattern. For example, in the 'Itch Game' each pupil would repeat what their neighbour had said and add their own contribution: 'This is _____ and she itches here; I am _____ and I itch here.' In another game, which was particularly successful at the start of the academic year, the pupils were expected to introduce themselves 'I am _____' with a comic action which would be copied by the rest of the group. On other occasions the pupils would be asked to express an opinion on a chosen subject. For example, pupils might be asked to comment on something, such as a series of pictures, displayed in the middle of the circle. Once again the emphasis was on every pupil having the opportunity to speak in turn. At this point in the lesson no value judgements were made about the quality of a pupil's contribution. Moreover, less confident pupils could, if they wished, simply repeat comments made by others.

During more open-ended discussions the pupils were often confused as to when it was their turn to speak and a pause, however short, would create an opportunity for the more vocal pupils to 'bully' their peers into answering. In order to overcome this difficulty and to ensure that individual pupils took some control of when and for how long they wanted to talk, an egg-shaped pebble was passed around the circle to indicate whose turn it was to speak. Only the person holding the pebble was allowed to speak whilst others had to listen. Here the rules also applied to me. In an attempt to provide a positive role model, I sat in the circle and participated in the same way as the pupils. Whatever form it took, the circle time was good fun and generated a great deal of good-humoured and shared laughter. However, in addition to the sheer enjoyment, the circle activities also fulfilled a number of important functions.

First, they ensured that every pupil spoke to, and was heard by, the rest of the class. Moreover, as the activities were tightly structured, an individual's contribution was expected both to be brief and to follow a predictable pattern. Having observed pupils sitting through whole lessons without speaking to either teacher or peers, I felt that these kinds of activities had an important role to play as ice-breakers. I believed that the difficulties which quiet pupils may experience in speaking in front of the whole class were likely to increase as the lesson continued. The circle activities ensured that every pupil heard the sound of their own voice within the first few minutes of the lesson.

Second, in addition to providing an opportunity to talk, the circle activities also ensured that all pupils had some experience of listening, or at least remaining silent, whilst others spoke. Participation in circle games gave me an ideal opportunity to stress the role of active listening in good discussions. Not surprisingly, vocal pupils who were used to dominating talk in the classroom experienced some difficulty in remembering to keep quiet at the appropriate times.

Incidentally, the experience of 'going round the circle' in order to hear everyone's point of view was used by the pupils to some effect during other small-group activities when they felt that their discussion was in danger of drying up. Several feedback sessions in which the pupils reported back to a larger group began with the pupils employing this strategy. Whilst the technique often seemed stilted and artificial, going round the circle to ask each person for their point of view often formed an important precursor to more naturalistic discussion which, in retrospect, could be seen to grow out of the initial statements. Finally, I felt that participation in the circle activities was likely to foster a sense of belonging to, and being accepted by, the class as a community. During my observations of mainstream class lessons this was the only occasion in which the whole class worked co-operatively and on equal terms. During other whole-class activities, such as preparing for a school assembly, the activity tended to be dominated by a small number of pupils.

Following the circle activities, and sometimes growing out of informal discussions, the rest of the lesson followed a clear and predictable pattern. In order to encourage pupils to talk about their personal experiences and attitudes I often began lessons with personal anecdotes of my own. For example, the subject of peer relationships was introduced by an account of my childhood friendships. I believed that the sharing of stories such as these would help to create a supportive environment in which pupils would be free to talk honestly about their own lives without fear of reprisals from others. So far as I am aware, I was totally successful in achieving this aim. During the course of my work with them the pupils discussed a wide variety of personal issues around the themes of family, friends and relationships. In all cases the other pupils were sensitive and supportive. I know of no instance in which individuals used information gained during the lessons to tease or bully others.

Having introduced the theme for the lesson I would then set a specific task for the pupils to complete with their talk partners. As with the withdrawal groups, pupils tended to like tightly structured activities in which there was a clear and easily attainable task. However, as the study developed the pupils became less apprehensive about tackling more open-ended tasks. For example, towards the end of the study Roxana and her partner had tremendous fun inventing appropriate characters to read the poem they had been asked to discuss. Similarly, Diana, Aberash and Mandy became quite 'carried away' by their involvement in role-play situations. Here, as elsewhere in the small-group activities, pupils demonstrated their willingness and ability to 'name their world' and make the learning their own.

Towards the end of the small-group activities the class would be told if, and in what form, they would be asked to report back to a larger group or the whole class. Depending on the nature of the task the feedback differed from lesson to lesson. If the task had been to participate in some form of role-play situation, then the pupils would be invited to 'perform' for the rest of the class. By comparison an open-ended discussion would be followed by a summary of the main points. Whilst the majority of the feedback activities involved oral work, on occasion pupils were asked to produce written evidence of what they had discussed in the form of charts or posters. In order to meet the specific needs of quiet withdrawn pupils I would make it clear whether the feedback was compulsory, and therefore expected from everyone, or purely voluntary. In this way I hoped to give them maximum opportunity to prepare themselves appropriately for what was to follow. Whilst I emphasized that I wanted as many pupils as possible to participate in the voluntary feedback, I never pressured reluctant pupils. I knew that, since many of the small-group discussions were taped, I would have access to their work even if they chose not to present it to the whole group.

Whether the feedback was voluntary or compulsory I emphasised that the audience response should always be positive and supportive. Sometimes, and in order to encourage the less confident pupils, I limited the response to three positive statements and only one constructive criticism. Where necessary I provided the positive statements myself. Interestingly, as I often pointed out to the pupils, there was never a shortage of pupils wanting to highlight the less successful aspect of other people's work. The fact that so many pupils were prepared to find fault with work done by their peers was justification enough for emphasizing the need for positive feedback. To conclude the lesson, the final circle activities would be either a summary of the main points of the lesson or, where that was inappropriate, games which emphasized the pleasure of working co-operatively.

In order to meet the specific needs of quiet pupils with emotional and behavioural difficulties, I was prepared to organize the lessons in a way which was both tightly structured and predictable. I felt this especially appropriate for this particular class, which had little or no experience of independent small-group work. As the pupils became more familiar with this approach and gained confidence in their own abilities it became possible to become more flexible.

Assessing pupils' talk

As part of the process of demonstrating the importance of talk for learning, I introduced the pupils to the idea of their assessing their own contribution to group discussions. This was done in two ways. First, I used episodes of talk recorded during previous lessons in order to demonstrate good practice. In this way pupils could be alerted to useful strategies such as asking appropriate questions and seeking clarification. In addition to providing good role models this activity also demonstrated that I did listen and take note of what was recorded during the lessons. It also gave me the opportunity to acknowledge good, thoughtful work. Here, as with the withdrawal groups, extensive use of tape-recorders was invaluable both in analysing episodes of talk and in emphasizing to the pupils the importance of talk for learning. Secondly, I asked pupils to complete evaluation sheets in which they ranked different aspects of their contribution to small-group discussions. These evaluation sheets were created by the pupils working in collaborative small groups. The groups began by drawing up a list of criteria which they thought were important for good or effective talk. Each group's contribution was added to a whole-class list and by a process of elimination these criteria were reduced to eight:

How well did I try to include others?
How well did I listen to other people's ideas?
How well did I express my feelings?
How well did I share my feelings?
How well did I show respect for other people's ideas and feelings?
Did I ask questions?
Did I use an appropriate level of voice?
Did I disagree with other people without putting them down?

These statements were reproduced on evaluation sheets. Pupils ranked each aspect of their contribution to specific lessons on a five-point scale. The evaluation concluded with the completion of the statement 'My general impression of the week's lesson is ...'. I felt that, especially in the early days of their use, these sheets served as a useful reminder of previous discussions about what constituted good or effective communication. As with other aspects of small-group work, the quiet pupils who had taken part in the withdrawal groups had some prior knowledge of a process of self-assessment and were therefore at a slight advantage over their normally more vocal peers. The fact that quiet pupils benefited in this way helped to further justify their participation in the withdrawal groups.

Pupil response

The effectiveness of using small-group activities can best be illustrated by reference to a particular lesson.

Following circle-time games as described above, the session developed with me introducing the subject of disability and more specifically the way in which children with disabilities are treated within our education system. Drawing on the recently televised film *My Left Foot* by Christy Brown and referring to the work of Stephen Hawking, I talked about the way in which stereotypical ideas about people with disabilities often emphasize the disability and ignore people's strengths and achievements. I then talked about the difficulties which families experience in trying to find mainstream school places for children with disabilities. Citing a particular example of a boy with multiple disabilities, I asked the pupils to consider whether or not such pupils would be better being educated in a mainstream school or a special school. I encouraged the children to draw on personal experiences and those of friends or family during their discussion.

The pupils were then given 15 minutes to work with their talk partners and, having arrived at a decision, be prepared to support this with as many reasons as possible. As usual, some groups were asked to tape-record their discussion. The pupils were told that on this occasion their feedback group would consist of three or four sets of talk partners and then the task would be to share what had been discussed. During the discussion I focused on observing the pupils and getting a sense of the nature and quality of their interactions. If I felt a group was flagging I suggested that they might consider what changes they would make to their own school to make it more accessible to pupils with different kinds of disabilities. In setting this task I hoped that the pupils would consider both the needs of pupils with disabilities and their own attitudes to those needs. At the end of fifteen minutes the class was organized into three feedback groups all of which were recorded. The success of this activity and the main features of this approach can best be illustrated through an examination of one pupil's contribution to the discussion.

First, as mentioned in the previous chapter, the initial work with talk partners gave Roxana the opportunity to practise telling her story to supportive friends before being faced with the large feedback group. Consequently, without any support beyond the opportunity to practise in advance, in the feedback group Roxana's account was far more structured and coherent. Thus telling her story in advance provided her with the opportunity to clarify for herself what it was she wanted to say.

Second, the earlier discussion with talk partners also provided pupils with something specific to contribute. In this case each pair had written a list of reasons why pupils with disabilities should be educated in mainstream schools. Admittedly the discussion began rather woodenly, with pupils taking it in turns to read from their list. In the transcripts which follow Roxana is indicated by the initials RC.

RC: Say one thing and then you pass round.
NM: No. Just say all of them.
SD: 'Cos they don't want people to feel sorry for them.
MS: They would like to be with people who have no disability.
NC: They want to be educated like us and be able to get a good job.

As the group continued talking, for a total of twenty minutes without intervention from a teacher, it was possible to see how the strategy of taking turns round the circle provided an opportunity for everyone to speak and formed an important starting point for the subsequent discussion. I am convinced that such strategies for initiating discussion should not be underestimated, especially as they can, as on this occasion, provide an opening for pupils to set their own agenda. When the pupils had introduced the topic by reading from their notes they began to swap anecdotes about disabled people they knew. Here, as in the rest of the transcript, Roxana played an active part in the discussion.

NM: Like my cousin, he's right funny and everything even though he can't walk, talk, use his hands or hear properly. He's still fun and you can play with him. If you leave him out he starts crying, so when we go there we always play together with him and his brothers.
RC: This boy on the end of my path, he's called Christopher and he's twelve. He's got a kind of disability and he's quite big and chubby. And he can't help himself, he eats all the time. Like once he went in the fridge and got this lard out and he ate it all and he didn't even get sick. He can do things like that. Like he'd been in the freezer and got some hard bread out and ate it.

Interestingly, the discussion became more animated when Roxana asked a question. This introduced a whole new dimension which seemed to have particular importance for her.

RC: Like say if you were pregnant and you'd just found out that if it were going to be disabled well like would you divorce it ...
OC: Abortion.
RC: have it abortioned like. What would you do Natasha?

It is significant that Roxana was so intent on finding an answer to her question that she hardly noticed when one of the other pupils corrected her terminology. As each of the pupils, including Natasha, a confident and accepted leader within the class, gave a negative response to this question, Roxana remained quiet. When it was her turn to speak she passed the debate to the next person in the circle.

NM: I would have my baby no matter what. You know my baby could come out with two heads like it could even be Siamese twins but I'd still have it.
RC: What do you think? What would you do?
MA: I'd have it.

It was only when Owen suggested an alternative answer that Roxana was prepared to suggest that an abortion might be a humane way to reduce suffering.

OC: If it were right brain-damaged and it couldn't do anything at all only sit there, and it couldn't see right ... I'd have it killed. [*Several girls say 'ah!'*]
OC: Life isn't worth living.
RC: No. Same with me right. I would like ... if it were really going to be in pain for the rest of its life I wouldn't have it because it's not really fair on it.
PP: It wouldn't be fair for it, suffering for all of its life.
NC: Yeah, but just think if you have a child ...
RC: But you wouldn't like your child to be in pain all through the rest of its life would you?

This illustrates Roxana's self-confidence in forming her own opinion despite strong peer group pressure, especially from Natasha, to conform. Moreover, whilst Roxana was not confident enough to openly contradict her friends, she was quick to develop Owen's suggestion, which suggests a growing confidence in her relationships with others. Even when the discussion became heated Roxana retained her self-confidence and continued to put forward her own point of view.

*   *   *

The episode of pupil talk discussed above illustrates many of the features of successful small-group discussions. The tone of the pupils' contributions and the way in which they support their views with anecdotes from their own experience suggests that they have been able to generate a genuine interest in the subject being discussed. In addition, by asking their own questions they control and direct the shape of the conversation. They are able to use their own language and experience in order to name their world. Moreover, the fact that they can disagree with each other and correct each other's mistakes without giving or taking offence suggests that, in this context, they have established warm and trusting relationships. In this chapter I have established that, with appropriate support from the teacher, small-group discussions can be extremely effective in encouraging quiet pupils to talk in school. Moreover, by allowing quiet pupils to work with known and trusted individuals, small-group activities can help them to gain confidence and develop relationships with their peers. In the next chapter I discuss how one-to-one interviews with pupils and parents can help to develop teacher–pupil relationships.

10 Talking with quiet pupils

As demonstrated in the previous two chapters, an important part of my work with the quiet pupils was the development and implementation of appropriate teaching strategies. Of equal importance were the series of one-to-one interviews I carried out with the pupils and their parents. These interviews were set up as a means of gathering data for my research. However, I soon realized their effectiveness in helping to establish relationships between teachers and 'hard to reach' quiet pupils. In this chapter I will discuss the importance of one-to-one interviews as a means of providing support for quiet withdrawn pupils. I will also explore the need for teachers to be alert to the fact that, in a minority of cases, quiet withdrawn behaviour can be a response to acute distress or abuse. I propose that, in addition to initiating dialogue between teachers and pupils, one-to-one interviews should be used to help to identify children who are in some way 'at risk' and in need of further specialized professional help.

The benefits of one-to-one interviews

Of all the research methods I employed in this research, it was the interviews which gave me most pleasure and which yielded the richest, most easily accessible data. Having the opportunity to talk with individual pupils and parents was a tremendous privilege. I am aware that this opportunity is not normally available to class teachers in the course of an ordinary school day. However, hearing pupils talk about their lives convinced me of the tremendous benefits to be gained from spending time with individual pupils and their families. Moreover, this approach of allowing pupils time and space in which to examine important issues is an important source of support for their emotional and social development. For quiet pupils it also provided an important forum for them to find their voice in the relative safety of a non-competitive environment. From a teaching perspective, one-to-one interviews are beneficial because they:

- provide pupils with an opportunity to talk about their experiences without having to compete with more vocal peers;
- provide teachers with an opportunity to spend time with, and get to know, pupils who are often overlooked in the classroom;
- provide teachers with important insights into the pupils' lives and experiences, which help to explain the quiet behaviour witnessed in school;
- provide an opportunity to forge relationships between pupils and teachers.

The development of good quality relationships in school, between teachers and pupils and among peers, is central to the process of empowering quiet pupils. Such relationships provide quiet pupils with feelings of security which allow them to take a more active role in their education. In a chapter entitled 'The Social and Emotional Context for Learning' Sally Beveridge (1993) acknowledges that the informal or 'hidden' curriculum of relationships and interactions at school can 'pose considerable demands on pupils with respect to their social competence and their personal resources, such as self-confidence' (p. 91).

In considering the qualities of an effective pupil–teacher relationship, it is generally accepted that pupils learn most effectively when they feel valued and secure, trust their teachers, and both understand and accept the full range of classroom demands (Pollard, 1988). Therefore a consideration of the social context and emotional climate for learning is important for all pupils. However, both the Warnock Report (DES, 1978) and the National Curriculum Council (1989) have argued that this may be particularly important for pupils with special educational needs.

Beveridge (1993) identifies a number of patterns of teacher behaviour which give rise to positive teacher–pupil relationships. These include: creating a climate of mutual respect; genuine interest in the pupils as individuals; care and concern for the class as a whole; and promoting pupils' self-esteem and motivation for learning through the provision of relevant and achievable tasks, and by regular constructive feedback and praise. One-to-one interviews have an important role to play in helping teachers to demonstrate their interest in the pupils as individuals. It is a way of demonstrating that individual pupils are valued, which can, of itself, help to promote pupils' self-esteem. One-to-one interviews can also be used to provide constructive feedback and praise.

In *Experiencing Special Education* (1993a) Barrie Wade and Maggie Moore begin their research account of the experiences of pupils with special educational needs with a summary of early studies of what children think about their teachers. These early studies (for example, Dale, 1967; Makins, 1969) emphasized the crucial importance of relationships for children. Moreover, the characteristics of a good teacher identified by pupils have as much to do with the personality of the teacher as with teaching abilities. Thus one study by Virginia Makins (1969) concluded that

> *how* children were taught matters more to them than *what* they are taught. Her sample placed emphasis on teachers who were lively and interesting, interested in their students and approachable. The main teaching ability mentioned was that of giving clear explanations to help understanding; the main dislike was shouting. [author's emphasis]   (Wade and Moore, 1993a, p. 29)

Wade and Moore's own research emphasizes the importance of relationships (between pupils, teachers and parents) for learning. It also emphasizes the frustration and anger experienced by pupils with special educational needs when their specific needs are over-emphasized or ignored. In both respects this research has clear implications for work with quiet withdrawn pupils in mainstream classrooms.

168

However, whilst positive relationships are essential in the education of quiet withdrawn pupils, there are times when such relationships are not, in themselves, sufficient. Similarly, whilst appropriate teaching strategies can go a long way to meeting the needs of the majority of quiet pupils, there are some pupils who need additional support at specific times in their lives. I see one-to-one interviews as an important part of a process of identifying the minority of pupils who may benefit from further specialist support. These pupils may be traumatized by the demands of school, prolonged bullying, alienation, family separation, illness, bereavement, violence or one of the many other difficulties which face children today. Before focusing on the needs of these children it is appropriate to provide an account of the one-to-one interviews I carried out with quiet pupils and their parents.

One-to-one interviews with pupils

During my work with quiet pupils I chose to carry out semi-structured interviews because they afforded an ideal opportunity for me to provide a context for the interview whilst, at the same time, allowing the interviewee to answer the questions in their own way and to introduce their own agenda if they so wished. My role was to provide a framework for discussion and then to listen carefully to what the pupils wanted to say. The emphasis on understanding the pupils' perspective through open-ended dialogue felt very different to the teacher–pupil interactions which I was used to. Indeed, they seemed to have more in common with counselling interviews in which I, the counsellor, listened with care and without judgement or prejudice to the thoughts and feelings of the pupils, the clients. This image was enhanced by the fact that the pupils used these interviews as a forum for discussing things that concerned them.

All the interviews with pupils, each of which lasted between 20 and 30 minutes, were tape-recorded and subsequently transcribed. They took place away from the classroom in places such as the music room and the library, which were both comfortable and relatively informal. Before the interviews I explained that the tape-recording would help me to think about the things that we talked about. I also said that the tapes were for my ears only but that I might need to talk to other people about the kinds of things we talked about. In this way I tried to offer the pupils some privacy without promising them confidentiality. I feel that this is an important distinction to make when working with young children. The interview schedules and examples of the transcriptions are included in Appendix 2 and Appendix 3 respectively.

Altogether I carried out four semi-structured interviews with each of the pupils. The first took place at the beginning of the study and focused on the pupils' interpretations of their life stories as portrayed on their personal time-line. These pictorial representations of significant events in the pupils' lives were produced as part of a whole-class activity prior to the interviews. These time-lines were important in allowing the pupils to have control over the content and style of our early discussions together. Once the pupils had exhausted their personal histories I tried to encourage them to think about their futures and especially about what they were likely to do whilst they were in school. In addition I asked pupils about how they saw themselves and whether or not they were talkative. These first interviews provided me with valuable information about the pupils' perceptions of their lives – past, present and future. They also formed the basis of subsequent interviews and work in both the withdrawal groups.

The second pupil interviews took place approximately four months later, that is, towards the end of my work with the pupils in withdrawal groups. These interviews began with an opportunity for the pupils to reflect back on the previous interview and all that had happened to them since. As a way of understanding their perceptions of themselves I also encouraged them to reflect on their school experiences during the previous academic year. Interestingly, whilst pupils were happy to talk about the kinds of work they had done during the year, they seemed to have difficulty in talking about what the teacher thought of their work. They also found it extremely difficult to predict what kind of things their class teacher was likely to write on their end of year report. Similarly, the pupils had little to say about their predictions for the following year. Using a class list as an *aide-mémoire*, the pupils were then asked to identify which pupils were clever, talkative, a good talker and a good listener. From this I encouraged the pupils to identify the characteristics which they associated with being a good talker and listener. The second interviews concluded with the pupils being asked to provide a description of themselves.

The third pupil interviews took place during the second year of the study (Phase Two) and ran concurrently with my teaching the quiet pupils in a whole-class context. As the focus of the third interviews was to provide pupils with an opportunity to raise any issues which they felt were important, they were asked about a variety of issues such as: 'Who is the most important person in you life?'; 'What makes you angry?' and 'What was your proudest moment?'. In addition to the questions which were asked of all the pupils, supplementary questions were asked of individual pupils about issues which they had raised previously. For example, Aberash was asked to elaborate on three points: her choice of pet; playing with her mother's things; and her view that shyness was natural. (Copies of the interview schedules are included in Appendix 2.) In contrast to the other interviews, in which I asked the questions, in this interview the questions were written on flash cards and chosen by the pupil in any order they wanted. This relatively minor change to the procedure ensured that the pupils were the ones who did the most talking, with me remaining quiet except to ask for clarification when necessary. Perhaps as a result of a number of factors (familiarity with being interviewed, a growing relationship with me, the type of questions being asked and the style of the interview) these interviews provided more personal reflection than had either of the two previous ones.

The fourth pupil interviews took place shortly after the

pupils moved to their secondary schools (Phase Three). These interviews focused on the pupils' perceptions of their new schools and how they felt they had adjusted to the new environment. In addition to finding out how the pupils had adapted to the different practical and academic challenges posed by their new schools, I was particularly interested in hearing about the relationships which the pupils had made both with teachers and with peers. In this interview pupils were asked to nominate up to three members of staff whom they felt it would be appropriate for me to approach for an interview. I felt that the pupils' reasons for their selection were as important as the selection itself.

Interviews with parents or significant others

Rather than assume that pupils came from traditional two-parent families, I began by asking the pupils to nominate someone at home whom I could approach for an interview. This gave them the opportunity to suggest either a parent or a significant other. In the event, eight pupils nominated their mother, two pupils nominated their father and two pupils nominated an elder sister as the best person for me to talk to. With one exception, everyone I approached agreed to take part in the interviews. Sadly Charlene's sister never kept any of the appointments I made with her.

As one of my reasons for interviewing parents or significant others was to establish their views of their children's education, it would have been inappropriate to assume that the interviewees were happy for me to conduct the interviews in school. I asked the interviewees where they would like to meet and as a result all but one of the 'parent' interviews took place in the pupils' homes. When asked where it was most convenient to meet, Aberash's mother said that it was easier for her to visit me for the first interview. The second interview took place in her office at work. The question as to where interviews should be held is not a trivial matter. My experience of interviewing parents in their own homes convinced me of the value of home visits in creating genuine dialogue between parents and teachers. For example, I learnt far more about individual pupils and the aspirations and values of their families during two home visits than I had previously learnt in a number of school-based parents' evenings. Away from school parents were far more honest about their children's education and about the community in which they lived than they were likely to be in the relatively alien environment of school. However, I do recognize that the notion of 'equal partnership' challenges the idea of the teacher as sole 'expert', a shift in emphasis which many teachers might be unhappy to accept.

The first parent interviews took place at the start of the study and focused on a discussion of their child's early development and experience of school. Whilst the interviews did include a direct question about the child's relationships within the family, much could be gleaned about the quality of parent–child relationships from the way in which the parents answered other questions. For example, the way in which Susie's dad spoke of the way in which she was 'dumped' on him suggested a degree of conflict in his relationship with his daughter which was later supported by Susie's decision to go and live with her mother. Similarly, the love which parents had for their children was often evident in the way in which the parents spoke of their children. Thus, in addition to providing important biographical information, these first parent interviews provided valuable insights into the quality of the parent–child relationships.

The second parent interviews took place towards the end of the study after the pupils had transferred to their secondary schools. I began asking parents to elaborate on specific issues raised by the first interviews. The interviews then focused on the child's transition to a new school, particularly the parents' reasons for choosing the school and their initial impressions of it. In order to provide a context for their comments about their child's education, the parents were also asked about their own experiences of school and especially about the ways in which they felt that they had been successful at school.

Need for further support

As I have already indicated, one-to-one interviews with pupils have an important role to play in providing support for quiet pupils. At one level it may be sufficient that the pupil has had the opportunity to voice their concern. For example, during small-group discussions Susie mentioned that her handicapped sibling had died shortly after birth. The fact that, despite having the opportunity, she never felt the need to mention this again suggests that either this brief reference was sufficient for her needs, or that she was not yet ready to discuss a potentially painful incident in her life. In either case support, beyond ensuring a sympathetic audience, would have been inappropriate.

A second level of support might be where individual pupils are given the opportunity to discuss issues in a one-to-one situation with the teacher or another appropriate person. My experience of work with quiet withdrawn pupils would suggest that these pupils benefit tremendously from private or small-group interactions. As my work has demonstrated, such pupils experience difficulties in talking freely in whole-class situations. Consequently, they need to be provided with the opportunity to voice their concerns in more private, non-competitive situations. During the course of this study I found the semi-structured interviews with pupils invaluable, both in providing them with the opportunity to voice their concerns and in supporting them whilst they planned coping strategies.

In carrying out these interviews I found knowledge and experience of Rogerian counselling techniques extremely useful in alerting me to the need to remain non-judgemental and non-directive. I believe that teachers would find training in counselling techniques helpful, but it may not be essential; after all, talking with pupils is an integral aspect of a teacher's role. However, as my observations suggest that teachers are more familiar with the experience of talking to, rather than listening to, pupils, I feel that such training would provide a useful theoretical and practical framework.

The biggest difficulty in implementing a counselling approach in schools would be finding sufficient non-contact time in which to conduct one-to-one interviews. I know that teachers work under tremendous pressures and that finding time to talk with individual pupils may not be a priority. In answer to this I would make three points. First, having private and uninterrupted time seems to be essential if quiet pupils are to feel sufficiently supported to begin to address issues of serious concern. As my experience has demonstrated, getting to know quiet withdrawn pupils can require a great deal of patient listening. Secondly, one-to-one interviews are not necessarily as time-consuming as one might imagine. The success of these interviews depends on the quality of the interaction, not on frequency, and unless pupils have specific and prolonged difficulties teachers could plan two sessions per pupil per year. This is probably significantly less time than teachers will spend disciplining or counselling loud potentially disruptive pupils. Finally, one-to-one interviews represent a useful and productive use of teacher time. In contrast to sessions spent disciplining unruly pupils, finding time to talk with quiet pupils is an extremely pleasant activity and one which is likely to produce positive feedback for both pupils and teachers.

The support discussed above can be provided by a class teacher without specific training or expertise. Class teachers can, and do, a great deal to offer pupils support. However, teachers also need to recognize those situations where their support is insufficient or inappropriate. I feel strongly that all professionals who work closely with children should be trained to identify the signs of potential child abuse or other forms of acute distress and be able to contact appropriate specialist support.

Moreover, I am aware that when it comes to the identification of acute or long-term needs, quiet withdrawn pupils are especially vulnerable. Whilst it is relatively easy to identify the emotional and behavioural difficulties of loud and potentially aggressive pupils, the special educational needs of quiet with-

drawn pupils can easily be overlooked. This is beautifully illustrated in the following case studies of two emotionally
disturbed children whom I taught during my first year of
teaching.

Case studies

These two case studies of emotionally disturbed pupils illustrate
the way in which aggressive and potentially violent behaviour is
easily identified by class teachers whilst quiet withdrawn
behaviour, and the causes for it, may go undetected.

The primary school in which I met Paul and Heather was in
an inner city area of high unemployment and associated
poverty. The school had a large proportion of pupils with
special educational needs, some of whom exhibited severe
emotional and behavioural difficulties. It is a sad reflection on
my initial training that, as a probationary teacher, I was ill-
prepared for the cultural shock of working with openly defiant
and deeply distressed youngsters. Paul's violent, aggressive and
often offensive behaviour drew attention to his needs, with the
result that much teacher time was devoted to offering support.
In sharp contrast, Heather's silence in the classroom meant
that no one in the school was aware that she was an abused
child. Heather's story is an extreme case; clearly quiet behaviour does not, of itself, indicate either physical or sexual abuse.
However, her experience serves as a useful signifier for the
quiet and compliant pupils who can so easily be overlooked.

Paul's story

Paul's reputation for aggressive behaviour preceded him. Even
so, it was difficult to come to terms with the fact that he spent
the first days of term on the classroom roof shouting obscen-
ities at the top of his voice. Whilst the staff could not condone
such behaviour they could, given his 'deprived home background', understand it. Understandably, individuals who
experience real hurt in early relationships with parents find it
difficult to risk further damage by entering into other rela-

tionships. Paul's reaction to his experience of maternal and paternal neglect and cruelty was to fight, with body and mind, anyone who came near. Reaching out to such pupils demands a great deal of time, patience and firm, even ruthless, love. (By 'ruthless', I mean a stubborn refusal to 'give up' on the pupil, even when they seem to reject any approaches made.)

Paul's teachers were divided as to what they thought was the appropriate support for pupils like Paul. Some wanted to work with them within mainstream education and offer stability in an otherwise turbulent life. Others thought that such pupils had specific emotional or psychological needs which would be better provided for in some form of 'special school'. A lack of coherence meant that Paul, and pupils like him, frequently had to deal with different kinds of response from individual members of staff.

Irrespective of where they are educated, the violent and aggressive language and behaviour of pupils like Paul force teachers to acknowledge, if not actually meet, their needs. Advice to the teaching profession on ways of handling disruptive, potentially aggressive pupil behaviour is well documented (for example, Rutter, 1975; Tattum, 1986; Wildake, 1986; Booth and Coulby, 1987), as are teachers' own accounts of critical incidents involving aggressive individuals (for example, Ball and Goodson, 1985; Nias, 1989).

However, as Heather's story illustrates, in the flurry of activity which typifies life in an inner city school, the needs of quiet or passive pupils are often overlooked, and specific emotional and psychological needs may go unrecognized.

Heather's story
In contrast with Paul, Heather was quiet and unassuming. She attended school regularly, completed her work adequately and despite experiencing some difficulties with academic work she caused no problems to school discipline. She would respond when I tried to talk with her about her schoolwork. However, she was extremely reluctant to talk or answer questions during whole-class discussions. In common with some of the quiet

withdrawn pupils highlighted in this book, Heather sat extremely still in class and showed little facial expression. She was a social isolate with few friends of her own age. She spent many, if not all, her playtimes watching other children play. She rarely attempted to join in with their games and was not automatically included in group activities. It was many years after she left primary school that Heather told me her horrendous life story.

For some years in early childhood Heather was sexually abused, first by her father and then by her stepfather. This was denied by her mother, to whom Heather naturally turned for help. Consequently, even as a small child, Heather was forced to face her situation alone. She 'coped' by bottling up her anxieties throughout primary school.

> But at the same time you're screaming inside and you're shouting at people inside and nobody can hear you and you can't really hear them because it's like because you're that far away inside yourself you like shut yourself off don't you, you bury yourself really really deep until you can't really see yourself or you can't really see out. And then it feels like you're shouting that much, it feels like you're going to explode and your head and your whole body will explode.

Heather's withdrawal and social isolation was her way of coping with the trauma of abuse. Her fear that she might explode and inflict harm on others meant that she had to keep tight control over her behaviour, 'You just hold it all in because I was scared of hurting somebody'. She talked about how she was 'screaming inside' and longing to be noticed by her primary school teachers. Implicit in this account of acute distress is the feeling that Heather considered herself in danger of becoming so withdrawn, so buried, that she would cease to exist at all.

Perhaps because she was unable to contain her anger any longer, when she transferred to secondary school Heather became loud, defiant and disruptive. Egged on by her classmates, she became verbally abusive to her teachers who tried to contain her behaviour with increasingly severe punishments. Heather was ashamed of the fact that, while she was at secondary school, she bullied several children (one of them viciously) over many years. Heather felt that she bullied this particular individual because she was frustrated by the girl's passivity and seeming helplessness.

On leaving school at 16 with no formal qualifications Heather rebelled; she left home to live rough on the streets and began a predictable, if not inevitable, downward spiral of drug abuse and crime. Some of her friends from that time have subsequently contracted AIDS from sharing contaminated needles. Heather was taken into care and spent some time living in hostels. At this stage in her life her self-image was so damaged that she prefaced even the most casual physical contact with the suggestion that she should not be touched because 'I contaminate people'. It was only during a period of probation for arson that Heather finally received the counselling support she so desperately needed. It has taken her nearly twenty years to begin to talk about the abuse she suffered as a child.

In so far as Heather is now receiving appropriate professional counselling and is beginning to build a new life for herself there is hope that her story might have a happier sequel. However, as her former class teacher, I am horrified that neither I nor my colleagues were aware of Heather's inner emotional turmoil. Because no one took the trouble to get to know this particular quiet and unassuming pupil, Heather's plight was not recognized. By denying Heather the opportunity to disclose the sexual abuse, neither her mother nor her teachers are entirely without blame. Andrew Wilkinson (1975, p. 95) pointed out that ignoring someone is in itself a form of abuse.

> There are various ways in which it is possible to damage human beings psychologically: by annoying them, insulting them, threatening them, persecuting them. But often it is far more effective to do none of these things: to do nothing to them, to leave them entirely alone. So in prison solitary confinement is recognised as a severe punishment.

There is a sense in which Heather's inability or unwillingness to make herself visible to her teachers unwittingly subjected her to a period of solitary confinement. A desire to prevent other quiet pupils from similar feelings of isolation is one of the motivations which underlie this book.

As I have already said, Heather's is an extreme case. Quiet behaviour does not, of itself, indicate physical or sexual abuse. However, her story illustrates the need for teachers to be aware that habitually quiet withdrawn behaviour can mask serious emotional trauma. As will be discussed in the next chapter, offering support to children who exhibit quiet withdrawn behaviour means being aware of and respecting their out-of-school lives. Sometimes this means tackling issues which are difficult, controversial, and/or outside the teacher's own experience.

11 Dealing with difficult issues

All my work with quiet pupils was directed towards giving them a voice in the classroom. I achieved this through small-group activities and one-to-one interviews with pupils and their parents. The success of this approach depended, at least in part, on allowing pupils and parents the opportunity to discuss personal, difficult and at times controversial issues and to have some control over the content of their discussion. During my work with quiet pupils they introduced a wide range of issues including bullying, child abuse, racism, drug abuse, terminal illness, death and abortion. Sometimes, as in the case of bullying, the issues had direct relevance to the pupils' experience of school. Other issues, such as abortion, generated interesting general debate. By drawing on comments from pupils, I was able to construct a personal and social education programme which covered issues which I knew to be of interest to them.

Accepting the pupils' agendas

As I have commented before, different groups of pupils developed their own ways of introducing their own agendas. Whilst the more vocal pupils would not hesitate to speak their mind and direct discussions, quiet withdrawn pupils would employ far more subtle means of 'naming their world'.

Darren was one of a group of boys in the class who appeared to show little hesitation about expressing his point of view; he was extremely vocal during discussions. During the course of my work with the class, Darren made a number of personal, relevant, and therefore extremely welcome, contributions which helped to shape subsequent discussions. In fact the statement about 'disagreeing with other people without putting them down' which was included on the pupil evaluation sheet (see Chapter Nine) originated from one of his comments. However, his direct approach was occasionally extremely disconcerting. For example, whilst using a picture as the stimulus for a story, Darren suddenly announced that his mother was extremely ill with cancer. I sought to empathize with him and offered what support I could in terms of time to talk with him about his mother's illness. Yet, despite my sympathy, I could not help but notice that there was something challenging, if not threatening, about the way in which he disclosed his concern. It was almost as if he were establishing barriers to exclude further communication. I felt very strongly that Darren would benefit from some form of bereavement counselling or therapy to help him to face his mother's illness and possible death.

Whilst confident pupils showed little hesitation about expressing their concerns, quiet pupils were far more reluctant to talk openly about their experiences. Consequently, in order to provide quiet pupils with a voice in the classroom, I introduced some of the sorts of issues and themes which the pupils had talked about during one-to-one interviews but were unlikely to raise themselves. Thus, there was often a clear link between the lessons and issues raised during one-to-one interviews with pupils. Obviously in making links between the interviews and the subjects of subsequent lessons I took extreme care to ensure that I was not betraying confidences. I never used material which could be traced to specific pupils. Similarly, I ensured anonymity by using appropriate pictures, poems or anecdotes of my own to introduce the themes for discussion.

One such incident occurred when Mandy's account of her friend stealing money in school led indirectly to a lesson in which pupils were invited to consider the range of options open to someone who suspected a friend of stealing. Whilst I never disclosed the original stimulus for the lesson, the ensuing discussion allowed Mandy the opportunity to discuss the issue and possible consequences with her friend. I do not think that the fact that a group of boys used the subsequent role-play exercise as a vehicle for talking about drug abuse, actually detracted from Mandy's opportunity to raise what was for her an issue of personal concern.

Similarly, Aberash's comments about playing with her mother's tool box led me to initiate a series of lessons in which the class were invited to explore stereotypical ideas about parents. Using the poem 'One Parent Family' by Moira Andrew I encouraged the pupils to consider how far they thought their parents fitted stereotypical images of parents. In the context of small-group discussions, Aberash was one of a group of pupils who were prepared to talk about the ways in which their parents differed from the stereotypes. In introducing this topic in this way I felt that I had helped to acknowledge Aberash's lived experience and give her a voice in the classroom.

Perhaps because they felt respected both by me and by their peers, there were a number of situations in which quiet pupils were prepared to introduce topics of their own. Possibly the most dramatic of these is the incident (discussed in Chapter Nine) in which Roxana wanted to discuss abortion. In addition to Roxana's growing confidence, it is important to note that it was during this exchange that Susie introduced the subject of the death of her own sibling: 'When my mum had me she had another baby but when it was two years old it died because it had brain damage.' It is possibly significant that her revelation was made at a time when noise in another part of the classroom made it difficult for the other pupils to hear what she had said.

As the examples above demonstrate, one of the features of allowing pupils a voice in the classroom is that they are likely to raise important, personal and often contentious issues. Talking with them and their parents can also, on occasion, reveal potential conflict either within the community or

183

between the values of home and school. A striking example of this were discussions about race and multicultural education.

Potential conflict

During the research both pupils and their parents spoke frankly about their experience of racism in school and in the local community. These open exchanges revealed deep tensions between the Afro-Caribbean, Asian and white communities. They also revealed areas of potential conflict between the values of school and those of the wider community. Aberash's parents spoke angrily of the racism which they experienced as members of the Afro-Caribbean community. They also spoke at some length about what they perceived to be institutional racism in the educational system. In their opinion their daughter's school was not going far enough in devising and implementing multicultural and anti-racist policies. By comparison, Mandy's mother spoke with contempt about the school's expectation that her daughter would learn about other cultures. The attitudes of these parents are discussed at length because they show how conflict in attitudes between home and school might contribute to quiet behaviour in school.

Aberash's family

Aberash's mother and stepfather were extremely critical of the school because, in their view, it had failed to implement what they saw as an anti-racist policy. Aberash's stepfather said,

> What's used to defuse the argument is multicultural education and 'let's do some bhaji, let's cook an Indian food, I'll wear a sari today, and that's multicultural education' – that is not multicultural education. Multicultural education is the culture that's multifaceted and unfortunately education in England is very one-sided, it's really a culture to satisfy whites' perspectives of black people.

Aberash's parents bemoaned the shortage of black teachers in school and believed that continual exposure to white images and value systems led to the Anglicization of children and a denial of their cultural roots. Her stepfather observed,

> There are certain inherent values that are reinforced through reading materials and within schools as a whole. There are no black staff in Aberash's school, therefore the majority of her social behaviour is shaped by white people, not black and that causes her to be very Anglicized and that will cause a clash when she comes home.

The potential conflict between the cultures of home and school can create a kind of 'double think' in which pupils maintain two conflicting images of themselves. However, attempts by staff to involve Aberash's mother and stepfather in addressing multicultural issues within the school met with limited success. It was clearly difficult for an all-white staff to deal with the sheer anger and frustration which Aberash's mother and stepfather articulated. It was also difficult for Aberash's parents to accept the role of unpaid workers in school. With some justification they argued that the way to ensure respect of black people and culture was to employ them as fully qualified staff with related authority and responsibilities.

Aberash's parents were critical of the school's definition of a multicultural policy. However, whilst they wanted to see the implementation of a curriculum which drew on many cultures and value systems they also wanted the school to be honest about the racism which is inherent in English society. As a black person growing up in Britain, Aberash's stepfather felt that his generation was taught more in school about the concept of inequality: 'Nowadays there's too much emphasis on equality in an unequal situation. You see it's taught at school that all races should live together not that all races don't or cannot.' There seemed to be conflict between the school's attempt to work towards racial harmony and equality and Aberash's stepfather's lived experience of racial disharmony within the larger society. In many aspects of life, for example housing, he felt that his family was defined by stereotypical assumptions related to his colour.

185

There's also another assumption that because black people are placed in the same context as white working-class, and the same analysis is put on the same response which is not true because in the Caribbean Aberash's family would not come from – they do not come from a working-class (inverted commas) background, but would come to this country and be suddenly told 'that's the context in which you're seen', so again there's a political context to me of Aberash's lack of communication … so Aberash's experiences are not in school, so therefore why should she have to respond in an institution that does not recognise her identity?

He linked Aberash's lack of communication in school with the fact that her culture was not represented, and by implication not valued, there. He felt that school did not meet Aberash's needs and that her parents have to compensate, spending time 'correcting things that really should be going on in school'. He suggested that Aberash liked being involved in oral work because it reinforced a black oral tradition. However, an alternative explanation might be that she simply enjoyed mixing with her peers and developing relationships which were discouraged by the extremely strident adherence to their own culture proposed by her parents.

Mandy's mother
Whilst Aberash's parents spoke at length and with some feeling about racism in education, Mandy's mother's comments were brief and extremely hesitant. This is probably because she felt embarrassed at expressing views which challenged the school's ethos. When asked why she had chosen a particular secondary school for Mandy she spoke of her reasons for rejecting the local comprehensive because of its multicultural policy. Her older children had experienced some trouble when they had attended the school and she wanted Mandy to have a better start to her secondary career.

I know it sounds wrong, but it's all for a certain culture of people down there. Because to be honest with you, I still believe the local comprehensive is for Pakistanis and all that because it's not for white children. They are trying to teach white children all about Pakistan. And for me it is all wrong. This is their country and they should be learning about their country and their standards.

Interestingly, one of the Asian families I interviewed also rejected this particular school because of its reputation for racial disharmony and lack of discipline. Rasheeda's mother was unhappy for her daughter to go to a school with a high Asian population 'because Asian children are always causing for trouble'. Moreover, Rasheeda's elder sister talked about her experience of the secondary school and how Asian children cared more about causing trouble than they did about their education: 'They used to, you know, swear in Pakistani, you know – rude and, er, used to get names and that's how the fight begins you see, you know all swearing or hitting somebody, you know telling somebody to hit you'. Clearly the local comprehensive had a poor reputation with both Asian and white families in the area. However, Mandy's mother's rejection of multicultural education went beyond criticism of a particular school. She objected to being asked to provide money for Eid celebrations in Mandy's primary school.

> I don't think it's right at all. I mean, if they come to live in this country they are supposed to live by our law, by our ways. Because we'd have to do it over there anyway. But I just don't like it. And there's no way I'd give Mandy money to pay for Eid. No way at all. I feel so strongly about it. Once or twice when there has been Eid I've kept Mandy off school. I mean she mixes with Asian children, she plays with them. I don't mind that. I just don't like her being pushed into learning about their ways.

Clearly Aberash and Mandy's families had completely different views about multicultural education. However, whilst neither group was happy with the provision made by the school, none of the parents I interviewed felt willing or able to discuss their concerns with the staff of the school. They seemed afraid to challenge the status quo and risk alienating the teachers. Whilst this makes for a significantly easier time for teachers, it also means that their relationships with parents

187

and consequently with pupils are based on a false premise that they share common opinions and ideals. This is hardly a firm foundation for education. Given the potential conflict between the values of home and school on the issues of racism it is little wonder that the school was experiencing some difficulty in reducing the incidence of racist behaviour between pupils.

In common with the majority of teachers, I tried hard to foster what I believed to be racially enlightened attitudes. However, real success in this area would only begin when the school adopted a whole-school policy which included dialogue with parents and other members of the community. One-to-one interviews and home visits appear to be particularly useful if parents, and indeed pupils, are to be able to talk frankly about their experiences and feelings. If such an approach were to be adopted then it would be important for schools to find ways of handling both implied criticism and the need for some degree of negotiation between parents and teachers.

Giving pupils and their parents a voice in the classroom is important in the development of child-centred education which aims to meet the needs of all pupils. However, despite the success of the programme as discussed in the previous three chapters, I am aware that teachers face a number of constraints which are likely to prevent them from adopting similar approaches in their classrooms.

First, there is what Robin Alexander (1984) has dubbed 'the primary ideology' which presupposes that children are innocent and have to be protected from the harsh realities of life.

Second, the pressures of the National Curriculum and the emphasis on the teaching of 'the basics' mean that teachers have little opportunity to develop the necessary curriculum initiatives such as personal and social education.

Finally, a child-centred approach in which children are encouraged to ask questions challenges the teachers' authority.

I will discuss each of these in turn.

Protecting children

There is a long-held belief in the inherent innocence of children and the need to protect them from the harsh realities of life (Alexander, 1984). However, I would argue that for many children the primary ideology which seeks to protect them from unpleasant aspects of life is doing them an acute disservice by denying their actual lived experiences. For example, of the twelve children highlighted by this book all but two had experienced separation from a significant other through divorce, separation or death. Similarly, all the pupils lived in an area noted for domestic and racist violence and drug-related crime. Where these issues are part of pupils' lived experiences they should not be denied by school.

> Crack exists and some of the biggest runners for crack and cocaine are eleven and twelve. They are not adults. Another issue is child abuse. There is a patronising way in which we talk to kids about child abuse, yet they go home and they get abused at home. It's like I've seen teachers talking about racism to black children in a way that makes them laugh. Teachers don't come out and talk about these issues as they really are.
>
> (Aberash's stepfather)

Ignoring issues such as drug abuse, or dealing with them in a patronizing way, is likely to alienate pupils and deny them the support they need to deal with potentially traumatic issues. Moreover, without a debate of these issues pupils have little opportunity to reflect on their lives and envisage alternative ways of being.

Nevertheless, the idea that pupils have a voice in their own education is fraught with tensions. Dialogue occurs between people who are prepared to meet as equals in a trusting relationship. This is extremely difficult for quiet pupils who may have a poor self-image and experience difficulties in forming and sustaining relationships. Moreover, inequalities are inherent in the school system. Even in the most liberal of classrooms pupils and teachers do not meet as equals. Teachers who wish to give credit to the existential experiences of their pupils are

189

constrained by their own standards and expectations and those of the school. Consequently, pupils and parents who wish to be accepted by the school learn not to disclose views which challenge the school ethos. Where the potential difference between the attitudes of home and school are not addressed pupils are compelled to hold two contradictory views in some kind of 'double think'. Moreover, the pressures of the National Curriculum mean that teachers are unlikely to have the time to deal with such contentious issues in the classroom.

The pressures of the National Curriculum

Without doubt the implementation of the National Curriculum highlights the importance of spoken language. Indeed, oracy is listed as one of the 'basics of learning' along with 'literacy, numeracy and a basic competence in the use of information technology' (Dearing, 1994, Section 2.9). However, whilst the 'back to basics' approach emphasizes the importance of developing oracy in schools, the prescriptive language of the curriculum orders implies a form of teacher-directed communication which prohibits pupils from 'taking possession of their learning' and 'making the learning their own'. As Ann Lewis (1991, p. 8) identified, this is linked to a contradiction which lies at the heart of the Education Reform Act. Sections 1 and 2 of the Act reflect contrasting approaches to aims and content in education.

> Section 1 is broad, referring to the need for a curriculum which promotes 'spiritual, moral, cultural, mental and physical development' and prepares pupils for the 'opportunities, responsibilities and experiences of adult life'. By contrast, Section 2 of the Act discusses the planned outlines of work in the discrete foundation subjects (plus RE).

Thus, Section 2 addresses only part of the aims given in Section 1; the broader aims are not met by the statutory programmes of study. In response to criticisms that the

190

programmes of study did not meet the broader aims of the National Curriculum, Dearing recommended that at Key Stages 1, 2 and 3 the Curriculum Orders should be slimmed down and less prescriptive. This would 'free some 20% of teaching time for use at the discretion of the school' (Dearing, 1994, Section 2.2). However, this does not necessarily release time for schools to develop curriculum initiatives such as personal and social education, as Dearing states in Section 2.4: 'The first priority for discretionary time must be to support work in the basics of literacy, oracy and numeracy. Beyond this, the bulk of the time released should be used for work in those National Curriculum subjects which the school chooses to explore in more depth.'

In a paper presented at the annual Association for the Study of Primary Education conference, Robin Alexander (1993, p. 3) expressed concern that an emphasis on the 'basics of learning' and a slimming down of the curriculum, as recommended by the Dearing report, would further marginalize some important subjects.

> Since the three core subjects (English, Maths and Science) are to be given protected status in this exercise, there is a clear implication that it is the non-core foundation subjects which are to lose most. They, and in particular art, music and PE, can least afford to be subject to further pruning.

In these terms Dearing's 'slimming down' cannot be seen as whole-curriculum thinking. It is merely a strategy for coping with the logistics of manageability while safeguarding the basics. Moreover, in his critique of the Education Reform Act (ERA), Robin Richardson has argued that the legislation will ensure that teachers are less able to broach controversial issues in the classroom because 'most of the time the new National Curriculum will prevent controversy arising' (1988, p. 21). As many contributors to *Children and Controversial Issues* (Carrington and Troyna, 1994) acknowledge, curricular initiatives in peace studies, sex education, multicultural/anti-racist education, anti-sexist education, political education and non-

191

competitive games have been parodied and dismissed as 'biased', even subversive and anathema to 'good' education. Against this background, the legitimation of the teaching of controversial issues in the early and middle years of pupils' schooling seems a long way off.

However, work with quiet withdrawn pupils suggests the need to safeguard those aspects of the curriculum which enhance the personal and social development of pupils. The need for pupils to leave the primary school with 'an appetite for learning and with a belief in themselves and their talents' is recognized by Dearing (1994, Section 3.12). What is not addressed in the report, nor in the Education Act which preceded it, is an acknowledgement that both appropriate curriculum objectives and enlightened teaching strategies have a vital role to play in the development of pupils' identities and self-esteem. Thus the pressure to raise standards in the 'basics' and deliver the nine subjects of the National Curriculum is likely to result in the marginalization of subjects such as personal and social education and with it the opportunities for child-centred education.

Challenging the teacher's authority

Another reason why teachers avoid dealing with difficult or controversial issues stems from a fear that pupils who are allowed to talk might 'answer back' and challenge the author-ity of the teacher. This is an issue which goes beyond important and sensitive issues of classroom discipline. When pupils are encouraged to ask questions, invariably they will raise subjects beyond the expertise of the teacher. Teachers are no longer able to maintain an image of themselves as the custodians of all knowledge. Whilst this image is, by defini-tion, both unrealistic and false, it protects individuals from addressing what they fear are their own inadequacies as a teacher.

The way in which teachers can be threatened by pupils' insa-tiable curiosity is illustrated in a poignant episode in *Petals of*

Blood, by Ngugi wa Thiong'o (1977). Godfrey Munira teaches in the village school. One day he takes his pupils out into the open air for a botany lesson in which he aims to provide the pupils with 'hands on' experiential learning. He teaches the children the names of the flowers and the names of their constituent parts and he feels proud to be imparting hard, factual, reliable information. But the fragile social order between himself and the children is maintained by nothing more substantial than his factual knowledge and his academic language. It begins to crumble when the children use vivid poetic metaphors to describe the flowers; when they notice that some flowers are worm-eaten, they ask disquieting questions about why beauty gets destroyed, and why God allows it to happen. His answer that it is all the laws of nature does not satisfy the children and they respond with formidable questions about humankind, law, God and nature:

> Man ... law ... God ... nature: he had never thought deeply about these things, and he swore that he would never again take the children to the fields. Enclosed in the four walls he was the master, aloof, dispensing knowledge to a concentration of faces looking up to him. There he could avoid being drawn in ... But out in the fields, outside the walls, he felt insecure.
>
> (Ngugi, 1977, p. 22)

Munira needs to learn how to handle passionate reflection, dialogue and argument amongst his learners, for learning cannot be confined to classrooms, to didactic instruction, and deferential note-taking. He also needs to risk himself in the pursuit of understanding.

Moreover, as the excerpt from *Petals of Blood* demonstrates, conversations with pupils force teachers to address uncomfortable issues and their own inadequacies in providing answers. Given that I was encouraging pupils to focus on the nature of relationships at home and in school, I anticipated that we would be covering some difficult issues including bereavement, family separation, bullying, racism and sexism. The fact that I had given some thought to these subjects helped

193

me to deal with the issues when they arose and to support pupils in ways which I thought were appropriate. However, because I was woefully unprepared, I found it difficult to deal with the subject of drug abuse which was introduced by a group of boys in a role-play intended to examine attitudes to theft. In the role-play, performed in front of the whole class, the boys demonstrated a disconcerting familiarity with the language and habits of drug abuse. The fact that neither I nor the school dealt adequately with the issue highlighted something of the possible conflict between the expectations of the teachers and the actual experiences of the pupils brought up in an area where drug-related crime was common.

Despite my concern that this subject had been raised in such a forceful way, I was prevented from developing the theme further. The head teacher explained that a discussion of drug abuse was an integral part of the school's health education programme and would be covered by the class teacher later in the year. The constraints place on me by the school prevented me from pursuing the pupils' agenda and I felt guilty that the pupils had not received the immediate support I felt they needed and deserved. This highlights the possible dangers of initiating open-ended discussion in a school which was inflexible in the way it presented particular issues. I felt this inflexibility wasted a useful opportunity to empathize with the pupils and to provide them with information to help them to understand what they saw and to empower them to make informed judgements about their own lives.

As this book has demonstrated, my desire to empower quiet pupils has led me to re-examine my own teaching. I have devised and implemented teaching strategies which help quiet pupils to develop their confidence in talking with and in front of others. My work in the classroom was enhanced by a greater understanding of the pupils' specific needs and of their relationships with parents, teachers and peers. In the next chapter I conclude with a summary of the main points raised by this book.

12 Summary points

This book began with the premise that habitually quiet non-participatory behaviour is detrimental to learning. In the introduction I suggested that such behaviour:

- prevents children from learning to express themselves (learning to talk);
- prevents children from asking questions and making the learning their own (learning through talk);
- prevents children from an active exploration of the subject being learned;
- prevents teachers from finding out what children know and thus monitoring and supporting learning;
- reinforces stereotypes, since girls, especially those with moderate learning difficulties, are more likely to exhibit quiet passive behaviour in the classroom than other groups of children;
- renders children invisible and can reinforce poor self-images;
- can be linked with social isolation and can make pupils vulnerable to bullying;
- can, in a minority of cases, mask serious emotional trauma such as bereavement, abuse, family separation, etc.

In Part One of the book I focused on the characteristics of quiet pupils and identified four types of quiet withdrawn behaviour. I also argued that recognizing the special educational needs of quiet pupils is an important precursor to empowering them to play a more active role in their education. In particular I established that :

- Quiet pupils experience anxieties about talking in school, especially in front of large groups of relative strangers.
- The anxiety that quiet children experience when asked to talk in

front of others clearly disadvantages them during whole-class discussions. Quiet pupils are often frustrated that their behaviour prevents them from making the most of the educational opportunities presented to them.

- Quiet pupils are aware that their behaviour puts them at a disadvantage in social situations where their inability or unwillingness to talk freely may be perceived as rudeness.
- Related to their anxieties about talk, quiet pupils also have difficulties in forming and sustaining relationships with peers. They also have poor relationships with teachers in school.
- Whilst the causes of quiet behaviour are complex, the behaviour of most quiet children followed a similar, and therefore predictable, pattern. In this book I have identified four types of withdrawal: 'being invisible', 'a refusal to participate', 'hesitation' and 'an inappropriate focus'.
- Whilst habitually quiet withdrawn behaviour is detrimental to learning and should be discouraged, it has to be recognized that for some pupils at least, occasional withdrawal may be the only way in which they can cope with overwhelming anxiety.
- In order to highlight the plight of quiet withdrawn pupils, it may be helpful to think of these pupils as having special educational needs. Recognizing their needs may be an important first step in empowering quiet pupils to play a more active role in their own education.
- Defining special educational needs is fraught with contradictions. The identification of need is likely to lead to the provision of appropriate support but may result in discriminatory labelling of individual pupils.
- In the majority of cases, meeting the special educational needs of quiet pupils is well within the scope of non-specialist class teachers.

In Part Two, which focused on the quality of parent–child relationships, I drew on recent accounts of John Bowlby's attachment theory to highlight possible connections between parent–child relationships and much of the quiet withdrawn behaviour witnessed in school. Given the recognized need for appropriate levels of separation and connectedness in relationships, I argued that there is a need for teachers to re-examine the quality of their relationships with parents and pupils. In particular teachers should recognize that:

- 'Good enough' relationships are those which provide children with an age-appropriate level of separation and attachment with parents or significant others who have become their attachment figures.

- Children who have 'good enough' relationships with their parents, or significant others, feel secure enough about their attachments within the family to be able to accept the transition to school without undue anxiety.

- Inappropriate parent–child relationships can be described as: 'overprotective attachment', 'confused attachment' or 'rejection'.

- An understanding of parent–child relationships may provide insights into a child's behaviour in school. However, care must be taken to ensure that psychological theories of attachment are not inappropriately applied.

- Whilst anxious attachments with parents may be the underlying cause of quiet withdrawn behaviour, pupil behaviour is also influenced by the quality of relationships in school. Throughout the book I provide evidence that supportive relationships (with teachers and peers) and appropriate teaching strategies can do much to encourage pupils to participate in the social and academic life of the classroom.

- There is a need to examine the ways in which stereotypical views, which regard nuclear two-parent families as the 'norm', may exclude or marginalize fathers and lone parents.

- There is a need to re-examine the ways in which parents are portrayed in school. It is important that textbooks and other teaching materials do not portray lone-parent families as a mutant form of the so-called 'normal' two-parent family. Similarly, teachers should be aware of how their own assumptions about parents and families could colour their expectations of the children they teach.

- There is a need to re-examine the way in which children are socialized in school. Enlightened practice should encourage children to develop all aspects of their personality and not limit them to traditional male or female roles.

- There is a need to re-examine the nature of teacher–pupil relationships and recognize that an appropriate balance of separation and connectedness is important for all pupils. However, being able to relate to, and feel connected with, teachers and peers may be a crucial precursor to learning for those pupils already silenced by what they perceive to be anxiety in relationships.

In the final part of the book I used my own experience of teaching quiet pupils to establish that:

- Meeting the needs of quiet pupils is entirely compatible with the objectives set out in the National Curriculum orders for Speaking and Listening.
- Small withdrawal groups can provide pupils with an opportunity to work with other quiet pupils and develop skills which they can practise in relative security before trying them out in a whole-class context.
- The criteria for appropriate withdrawal from the mainstream classroom should be that it is short, temporary and has a specific focus.
- In a whole-class context, structured but open-ended co-operative small-group activities can be extremely effective in increasing the amount of pupil talk and providing pupils with some autonomy over their learning.
- Small-group activities provide the teacher with the opportunity to stand back and reflect on the nature and quality of interactions between pupils.
- 'Talk partners' provide pupils with the security they need if they are to participate in classroom discussions. Talking with known and trusted individuals also provides pupils with an opportunity to practise or rehearse what they want to say.
- When focusing on talk as the subject for discussion and the medium for learning, teachers need to identify the characteristics of successful talk and make these explicit to children.
- Through use of simple evaluation sheets and recorded episodes of talk, children can be encouraged to reflect on the quality of their own discussions.
- One-to-one interviews are invaluable in that they provide pupils with an opportunity to talk about their experiences without having to compete with more vocal peers.
- One-to-one interviews provide teachers with an opportunity to spend time with, and get to know, pupils who are often over-looked in the classroom.
- Whilst appropriate teaching strategies can meet the special educational needs of many quiet pupils, it has to be recognized that some pupils are so damaged by their life experiences that they need the additional support of some form of counselling or therapy.

- Empowering quiet pupils involves encouraging them to talk about their experiences in the classroom. In order to do this teachers have to be prepared to acknowledge and respect their pupils' out-of-school experiences.
- Teachers wishing to empower quiet pupils have to be prepared to deal with and respond appropriately to a number of issues which may be outside their personal experience and which they will consequently find challenging.

*   *   *

I hope that this book will help to highlight the plight of pupils who habitually exhibit quiet withdrawn behaviour, and inspire others to find ways of meeting their needs. To echo the quote at the beginning of the book, education should aim to reach the unreached and include the excluded.

References

Adams, C. (1988) 'Gender, race and class: essential issues for comprehensive education', in Chitty, C. (ed.) *Redefining the Comprehensive Experience*. Bedford Way Papers 32, London: University of London Institute of Education.

Ainscow, M. and Muncey, J. (1989) *Meeting Individual Needs*. London: David Fulton.

Ainscow, M. and Tweddle, D. (1988) *Encouraging Classroom Success*. London: David Fulton.

Ainsworth, M.D.S. (1967) *Infancy in Uganda: Infant Care and the Growth of Attachment*. Baltimore: Johns Hopkins Press.

Alexander, R. (1984) *Primary Teaching*. London: Holt, Rinehart and Winston.

Alexander, R. (1993) 'What primary curriculum? Dearing and beyond'. Paper presented at the 6th National Conference of the Association for the Study of Primary Education, York.

Apter, T. (1985) *Why Women Don't Have Wives*. London: Macmillan.

Arcana, J. (1981) (first pub. 1979) *Our Mothers' Daughters*. London: Women's Press.

Arcana, J. (1983) *Every Mother's Son*. London: Women's Press.

Ashley, B. (1977) *The Trouble with Donovan Croft*. Harmondsworth: Penguin.

Ball, S. J. and Goodson, I. F. (eds) (1985) *Teachers' Lives and Careers*. Lewes: Falmer.

Bandman, B. (1973) 'Do children have any natural rights?' in Roaf, C. and Bines, H. (eds) (1989) *Needs, Rights and Opportunities*. London: Falmer.

Barnes, D. (1979) (first pub. 1976) *From Communication to Curriculum*. Harmondsworth: Penguin.

Barrett, M. and Trevitt, J. (1991) *Attachment Behaviour and the Schoolchild*. London: Routledge

Barton, L. (ed.) (1988) *The Politics of Special Educational Needs*. London: Falmer.

Bell, J. (1987) *Doing Your Research Project*. Milton Keynes: Open University Press.

Benjamin, J. (1990) (first pub. 1988) *The Bonds of Love*. London: Virago

Beveridge, S. (1993) *Special Educational Needs in Schools*. London: Routledge.

Booth, T. and Coulby, D. (eds) (1987) *Producing and Reducing Disaffection*. Milton Keynes: Open University Press.

Bowlby, J. (1977) 'The making and breaking of affectional bonds: 1. Aetiology and psychopathology in the light of attachment theory' *British Journal of Psychiatry*, **130**, pp. 201–10.

Bowlby, J. (1989a) (first pub. 1979) *The Making and Breaking of Affectional Bonds*. London: Routledge.

Bowlby, J. (1989b) (first published 1969) *Attachment and Loss: Vol 1*. London: Pelican Books.

Braten, S. (1992) 'Born with the other in mind'. Paper presented at the 7th International Educational Therapy Conference, Oslo.

Brown, C. (1989) (first pub. 1954) *My Left Foot*. Reading: Cox & Wyman.

Byrne, E.M. (1985) 'Equality or equity? a European overview', in Arnot, M. (ed.) *Race and Gender: Equal Opportunities Policies in Education*. Oxford: Pergamon.

Carrington, B. and Troyna, B. (eds) (1994) *Children and Controversial Issues: Strategies for the Early and Middle Years of Schooling*. London: Falmer.

Cazden, C. B. (1988) *Classroom Discourse*. London: Heinemann.

Chester, P. (1990) *Sacred Bond*. London: Virago.

Children Act (1989) London: HMSO.

Chodorow, N. (1978) *The Reproduction of Mothering*. London: University of California Press.

Cline, S. and Spender, D. (1987) *Reflecting Men at Twice Their Natural Size*. London: Deutsch.

Collins, S. (1991) 'Transition from lone-parent family to step-family' in Hardey, M. and Crow, G. (eds) *Lone Parenthood*. London: Harvester Wheatsheaf.

Cooper, P. (1993) *Effective Schools for Disaffected Students*. London: Routledge.

Croll, P. and Moses, D. (1985) *One in Five: The Assessment and Incidence of Special Educational Needs*. London: Routledge & Kegan Paul.

Dale, R.R. (1967) 'Teachers who have had a bad influence', *Education for Teaching*, **74**, pp. 25–32.

Dearing, Sir Ron (1994) *The National Curriculum and its Assessment: Final Report*. London: SCAA.

DES (1978) *Special Educational Needs* (Warnock Report). London: HMSO.

201

DES (1981) *Education Act*. London: HMSO.
DES & WO (1990) *English in the National Curriculum*. London: HMSO.
DFE (1993) *Education Act*. London: HMSO
DFE (1995) *National Curriculum Orders for English*. London: HMSO.
Eichenbaum, L. and Orbach, S. (1985) *Understanding Women*. London: Penguin.
Elshtain, J. B. (1981) *Public Man, Private Woman*. London: Penguin.
Evetts, J. (1973) *The Sociology of Educational Ideas*. London: Methuen.
Fish, J. (1989) *What is Special Education?* Milton Keynes: Open University Press.
Ford, J., Mongon, D. and Whelan, M. (1982) *Special Education and Social Control*. London: Routledge & Kegan Paul.
Freeman, M. (1987) 'Taking children's rights seriously', *Children and Society*, 1 (4), pp. 229–319.
Freire, P. (1972) *Pedagogy of the Oppressed*. London: Sheed & Ward.
Gilligan, C. (1982) *In a Different Voice: Psychological Theory and Women's Development*. London: Harvard University Press.
Glendenings, C. and Millar, J. (eds) (1987) *Women and Poverty in Britain*. Brighton: Wheatsheaf.
Guntrip, H. (1968) *Schizoid Phenomena: Object Relations and the Self*. London: Hogarth Press.
Hardey, M. and Crow, G. (eds) (1991) *Lone Parenthood*. London: Harvester Wheatsheaf.
Horney, K. (1939) *New Ways in Psychoanalysis*. London: Routledge & Kegan Paul.
Horney, K. (1945) *Our Inner Conflicts*. London: Norton.
ILEA (1985) *Educational Opportunities for All?* (Fish Report). London: ILEA.
Lamb, M. E., Pleck, J. J. and Levine, J. A. (1987) 'Effects of increased paternal involvement on fathers and mothers', in Lewis, C. and O'Brien, M. (eds) *Reassessing Fatherhood*. London: Sage.
Laslett, P. (1982) 'Foreword' in Rapoport, R.N, Fogarty, M. P. and Rapoport, R. (eds) *Families in Britain*. London: Routledge & Kegan Paul.
Leonard, D. and Speakman, M. (1986) 'Women in the family: companions or caretakers?' in Beechey, V. and Whitelegg, E. (eds) *Women in Britain Today*. Milton Keynes : Open University Press.
Lewis, A. (1991) *Primary Special Needs and the National Curriculum*. London: Sage.
Lewis, C. and O'Brien, M. (1987) *Reassessing Fatherhood*. London: Sage.
Lynch, M. (1986) *Multicultural Education: Principles and Practice*. London: Routledge & Kegan Paul.
McCormack, M. (1990) *Divorce and After: Fathers' Tales*. London: Macdonald.

Main, M. and Weston, D. (1981) 'The quality of the toddler's relationship to mother and father: related to conflict behaviour and the readiness to establish new relationships', *Child Development*, 52, pp. 932–40.

Makins, V. (1969) 'Child's eye view of teacher', *Times Educational Supplement*, 19 September, pp. 21–23.

Mercer, N. (1995) *The Guided Construction of Knowledge: Talk Amongst Teachers and Learners*. Clevedon: Multilingual Matters.

Mitchell, A. (1985) *Children in the Middle: Living Through Divorce*. London: Tavistock.

Morris, J. (ed.) (1992) *Alone Together*. London: Women's Press.

Mortimore, P., Sammons, P., Ecob, R. and Stoll, L. (1988) *School Matters: The Junior Years*. Wells: Open Books.

Murray, L. (1992) How learning is impaired in babies whose mothers have postnatal depression. Paper presented at the 7th International Educational Therapy Conference, Oslo.

National Curriculum Council (1989) *Curriculum Guidance 2: A Curriculum for All*. York: NCC.

Ngugi wa Thiong'o (1977) *Petals of Blood*. London: Cox & Wyman.

Nias, J. (1989) *Primary Teachers Talking*. London: Routledge.

Nice, V. E. (1992) *Mothers and Daughters: A Distortion of a Relationship*. London: Macmillan.

O'Brien, M. (1987) 'Patterns of kinship among lone fathers', in Lewis, C. and O'Brien, M. (eds) *Reassessing Fatherhood*. London: Sage.

Oliver, M. (1988) 'The social and political context of education policy', in Barton, L. (ed.) *The Politics of Special Education*. London: Falmer.

Olivier, C. (1989) *Jocasta's Children*. London: Routledge.

Pederson, F. A. (1980) *The Father–Infant Relationship*. New York: Praeger.

Piontelli, A. (1992) *From Fetus to Child*. London: Routledge.

Pirani, A. (1989) (first pub. 1988) *The Absent Father: Crisis and Creativity*. London: Arkana.

Pollard, A. (1988) 'The social context of special needs in classrooms', in Thomas, G. and Feiler, A. (eds) *Planning for Special Needs: A Whole School Approach*. Oxford: Blackwell.

Potts, P. (1986) Equal opportunities: the fourth dimension, *Forum for the Discussion of New Trends in Education*, 29 (1), pp. 13–15.

Pye, J. (1989) (first pub. 1988) *Invisible Children*. Oxford: Oxford University Press.

Race Relations Act (1976) London: HMSO.

Renvoize, J. (1985) *Going Solo: Single Mother by Choice*. London: Routledge & Kegan Paul.

Reynolds, D. and Cuttance, P. (eds) (1992) *School Effectiveness: Research, Policy and Practice*. London: Cassell.

203

Rich, A. (1992) (first pub. 1976) *Of Woman Born: Motherhood as Experience and Institution*. London: Virago.

Richardson, R. (1988) 'The right approach', *New Internationalist*, February, p. 11.

Roaf, C. and Bines, H. (eds) (1989) *Needs, Rights and Opportunities: Developing Approaches to Special Education*. Lewes: Falmer.

Rutter, M. (1975) *Helping Troubled Children*. Harmondsworth: Penguin Education.

Sex Discrimination Act (1975) London: HMSO.

Shaw, S. (1991) 'The conflicting experiences of lone parenthood', in Hardey, M. and Crow, G. (eds) *Lone Parenthood*. London: Harvester Wheatsheaf.

Smith, D. (1990) *Stepmothering*. Hemel Hempstead: Harvester Wheatsheaf.

Statham, J. (1986) *Daughters and Sons : Experiences of Non-sexist Child Raising*. Oxford: Blackwell.

Straker-Welds, M. (ed.) (1984) *Education for a Multicultural Society*. London: Bell and Hyman.

Sutherland, A. (1981) *Disabled We Stand*. London: Souvenir Press.

Tattum, D. P. (ed.) (1986) *Management of Disruptive Pupil Behaviour in Schools*. Chichester: Wiley.

Tizard, B. and Hughes, M. (1984) *Young Children Learning*. London: Fontana.

Tomlinson, S. (1982) *The Sociology of Special Education*. London: Routledge & Kegan Paul.

Wade, B. and Moore, M. (1993a) *Experiencing Special Education*. Buckingham: Open University Press.

Wade, B. and Moore, M. (1993b) *The Promise of Reading Recovery*. London: Education Review Publications.

Widlake, P. (1984) *How to Reach the Hard to Teach*. Milton Keynes: Open University Press.

Widlake, P. (1986) *Reducing Educational Disadvantage*. Milton Keynes: Open University Press.

Wilkinson, A. (1975) *Language and Education*. Oxford: Oxford University Press.

Wray, D. and Medwell, J. (1991) *Literacy and Language in the Primary Years*. London: Routledge.

Young, D. (1984) *Knowing How and Knowing That*. London: Birkbeck College.

Appendix 1: Interviews and observations

The data consisted of: semi-structured interviews with pupils, parents and teachers; observations of classroom interactions in both primary and secondary schools; and observations of small-group interactions in both withdrawal groups and as part of whole-class teaching.

During the study I carried out 45 interviews with the pupils, 22 with parents and ten with secondary school teachers. The interviews usually lasted between 30 and 45 minutes. All were taped and transcribed (there were approximately 40 hours of tapes and 500 pages of transcripts).

I spent ten hours observing the pupils in their primary classrooms. Opportunities to observe secondary pupils differed considerably from school to school. For example, I had no difficulty in gaining permission to shadow Justina throughout the school day. In other schools access was more restricted and had to be limited to two hours of lessons. Despite these restrictions, during the course of the study I spent over twenty hours observing the pupils at work in their secondary schools, a total of more than thirty classroom observation hours.

Teaching the pupils (in withdrawal groups during Phase One and in a whole-class context in Phase Two) occupied over 35 hours. In addition to recording my observations in a 'teacher's journal', I also tape-recorded hundreds of episodes of talk. Whilst some of these have been transcribed for analysis, this aspect of my research generated far more data than it was possible to analyse in a study of this length. Whilst appreciating the advantages of recording small-group discussions, I learned the hard way to be more selective in my use of tape-recorders in the classroom.

In addition to the data discussed above, informal conversations with pupils, teachers and parents provided important insights to my understanding of the pupils' experiences. I also got into the habit of recording my own, often very private, reflections in my teacher's journal. In this way my teacher's journal became a record of both the progress of the project and developments in my own thinking.

Appendix 2: Interview schedules

First pupil interview

Life Line

Tell me about your life line.

What are the important events?

Tell me about your family.

How many brothers and sisters do you have?

Future

Which school do you want to go to? Why?

What job would you like to do?

What family do you think you would like?

Where would you like to live?

School

Which lessons do you like best? Why?

Which lessons do you like least? Why?

What are you best at?

What would you like to be better at?

Talk

Would you describe yourself as a talkative person?

Do you talk much in class?

Do you talk much at home?

Who do you talk to most?

What kind of things do you talk about?

Who do you talk to about problems?

Shyness

Would you describe yourself as a shy person?

When do you feel shy?

What is it like if you feel shy?

How do you overcome your shyness?

What is the opposite of being shy?

When do you/what makes you feel confident?

(Note: Provide opportunities for pupils to add any comments that they might wish to make.)

Second pupil interview

This Year

What have you done since the first interview? At home ... At school ...

What have you learned/got better at?

What has been your biggest success/disappointment?

What would your like your report to say at the end of the year?

What do you think your report will say?

How do you feel about next year? How will it differ from this year?

The Class

Looking at the class list, who do you think

is the cleverest in the class? Why?

talks most?

talks least?

is the best talker in the class?

is the best listener in the class?

What makes a good talker?

What makes a good listener?

Yourself

Are you a good talker/listener?

Is there anything about your behaviour that you are trying to change? Why?

How would you describe yourself?

(Note: Provide opportunities for pupils to add any comments that they might wish to make.)

Third pupil interview

If you were interviewing me what questions would you ask?

How can we improve the 'Thursday Morning Talk Back' sessions?

If you had three wishes what would you wish for?

Who is the most important person in your life?

What makes you angry?

What makes you happy?

Do you remember any of your dreams? What are they?

Is there anything that scares you?

Have you ever done anything that you were ashamed of?

What was your proudest moment?

(Questions were written on individual cards and answered in whatever order the pupil chose.)

Additional questions: specific to each individual pupil

Mandy

How do you feel about Massaret joining your group on Thursday mornings?

How are you getting on with your maths now?

Do you enjoy acting out your plays on Thursday mornings?

Diana

Do you enjoy acting out your plays on Thursday mornings?

What would you like Dawn to do in the future?

Justina

One week you said something about a 'proper family'. What is a proper family?

You also talked about a 'respectable mother'. What did you mean?

Aberash

You said that you would like a panther as a pet. Why?

Please explain what you meant when you said you played with your mum's things.

You said shyness is natural. Can you explain a bit more about what you meant?

Vicky

What is your new house like?

Why did you change schools?

What is your new school like?

Pete

What do you do in your spare time?

Tell me about your pets.

Tell me about your brother and sister. What are they like?

Susie

What do you do in your spare time?

Has Denise got any children of her own?

Tell me about them.

Roxana

What do you do in your spare time?

Tell me about your brother's band.

Duncan

Tell me about your brothers. How do you get on with them?

Have you made anything recently?

Pamela

What advice would you give to someone who was going to live apart from someone who had been very close?

How is your sister?

Tell me about the painting you do with your father.

Charlene

Last time we talked you complained that your brother was misbehaving at school. How are things now?

Tell me about your mum.

Rasheeda

I've missed you. Tell me about what you have been doing.

Has your sister had her baby yet?

(Note: Provide opportunities for pupils to add any comments that they might wish to make.)

Fourth pupil interview

1 The last time we met you were at primary school. When did you move to this school?
How did you feel about starting secondary school?
What made you choose this particular school?

2 What were the first days at this school like?
How have you settled down since?
What do you particularly like/dislike about this school?
(Note: try to cover both social and academic aspects.)

3 Tell me about your friends in this school.
Do you still see people from your primary school?

4 Which lessons do you like/dislike? Why?
    "   "   are you most successful in?
    "   "   are you doing for the first time?
Do you have homework? How do you feel about it?

5 Have you got to know any teachers particularly well?
Do you feel that there are some teachers who do not know you very well yet?
(Note: amount and type of contact – that is pastoral/academic; subject; status; sex and age of teacher, teaching style.)

Who is the best person for me to talk to about you and your progress in this school?

1st   2nd   3rd

6 In the last two years at primary school you were taught by Mr N_____.
What do you remember about that school? How does this school compare with your primary school? In what ways is it the same/different/better/worse?

(Note: Provide opportunities for pupils to add any comments that they might wish to make.)

First parent inerview

Factual data

Date of birth

Place of birth

Number of siblings

Relationship with siblings

Early years

What was she like as a baby?

When did she start walking, talking, etc?

How did you encourage her?

What kind of things could she do before starting school?

Did you/do you read to her?

First school

Whcn? Where?

How did she feel about going to school?

How well did she get on with other children?

How did she find the lessons?

What kind of things did the teachers say about her?

Middle school

What kind of things did she say about moving to a new school?

What were her main concerns?

How did she take to the change when it happened?

Current feelings about school

How much does she talk about school?

What does she say about school?

What are her favourite/best subjects?

What does she dislike?

Which subjects need to be improved?

How does she get on with teachers/other pupils in school?

Relationships

Who in the family is she closest to?

How does she get on with adults and other children outside the immediate family?

Tell me about her out of school friends.

Future

What kind of future do you envisage for her?

What does she say about her future ... education/occupation/family life?

Are there any other major events or people that have had a significant effect on her?

Summary

How would you describe your daughter?

Is there anything else you would like to add (or ask)?

Second parent interviews

1 Explore issues arising from first interview. Subject specific to each individual.

2 Your daughter is now at _____ school. Why did you choose that particular school?

(Note how influential were:
  other parents
  other children/friendship groups
  the school's reputation
  geographical location.)

3 What are your first impressions of the school?
  What impressions do you get from talking to other parents and children?

Appendix 3: An interview transcript

Diana: First interview

JC: Right, Diana. The first question is: can you tell me about your life-line? What have you got on there?

D: When I was four years old my sister was born and I was on holiday when it happened so we had to come down, we had to come home a week earlier to see my sister. Er ...

JC: So who were you on holiday with?

D: My auntie and my dad and that's all.

JC: Mm.

D: When I were five ...

JC: Let's go back to your sister a little bit. What's your sister called?

D: Dina. She were so small that she had to go into an incubator only for a couple of weeks and now she's all right.

JC: And how did you feel when she was born?

D: Happy. [Pause]

JC: And do you get on well together?

D: She's a bit small for her age but ... she's six and she's about ... about as high as ... you know little Gavin in the first year, she's a lot smaller than him and she's six.

JC: Mm.

JC: Right: would you like to tell me the rest?

D: When I were five I went to Spain 'cos my auntie lives in Spain. We went to see her because ... she'd just got married ...

JC: Mm ...

D: ... and I had to wear this right pink dress and it looked awful on me.

JC: Were you a bridesmaid?

D: Yeah. I started school when I were five an' all and it was quite strange because it were like ... in those schools, right, when you first start it's really strange to you ...

JC: Mm.

D: ... and ... when ... it were when I came back from Spain that I

started school and everybody ... and the teacher knew that I had
been in Spain and everyone were saying, 'what were it like in
Spain?' and things like that.

JC: Did you like Spain? Would you like to go ...

D: I'd like ... I might be going again ...

JC: Are you looking forward to that?

D: Yeah.

JC: What's the thing about Spain you like best?

D: Er ... beach ...

JC: Mm.

D: ... and ... hotels were nice because my auntie were like living in
a hotel before she got a house and when she got her house ... a
house ... she sent a photograph back to Britain what it were like
and it were really big and since that she's had two children,
Jonathan and Amanda.

JC: Mm. [Pause]

JC: What happened next then on your time line?

D: When I was six I went to France ...

JC: Mm.

D: ... 'cause my dad thought we should have a little holiday, but when
we got to France I didn't like it that much because you know when
like you go shopping in France there's all these people who start
pushing and everything, and I nearly got lost.

JC: Mm.

D: ... and you know ...

JC: Was that scary?

D: ... 'cos everybody ... like if you see advertisements on telly where
all them French people ... and things and they're all pushing ...
and pull things because they want to get to the shop and everything and people, they say, 'oh well, it's a bit better than that in
Sp ... in France'. But it's true I think, they all do that and that ...
and I saw a little baby, she were lost ... [Pause]

D: ... oh yeah, and when I came back from Spain ... I mean France
– my mum didn't go – and Dina ... were about ... how old were
she now ... she'd been two years old and she ... like when I got
back she came running up to me going 'Diana, Diana'.

JC: She was excited to see you after all that time?

D: I went for four weeks.

JC: Four weeks? That's a long time, isn't it?

D: Er and when I were seven I went to Scarborough with my uncle,
my auntie, my nanan and my grandad, my four cousins, my dad,
my mum, my sister and we had loads of fish n' chips ...
(*Laughter*)

D: ... and it were really silly and when we went on the beach, right, my cousin was trying to bury us all and you know like you do ... and then sands just above their head I did it and she couldn't get out after all that ... er ... then when we got back from Scarborough, right, and we went to my other nanan's and she said that when she went to Scarborough when she were small it were really, really cold ...

JC: Mm.

D: ... and all waves, right, they were like bashing rocks and everything ... and when we were at Scarborough ... we ... you know at night like when you go to pub and disco we met a girl and she said last time she came to Scarborough somebody fell off of one of rocks and went down into sea when she ... when it were in the middle, well not in the middle of the night when sea comes in but she didn't drown.

JC: Well, that's good then, isn't it?

D: When I were eight I broke my leg and I had to go to hospital ... 'cause I were playing on this like ... what do you call them ... have you seen them new bikes that have just come out with those rubber tyres? Well I were playing on one of them but it were like one of them old ones and I fell down this like little ramp thing and I broke my leg.

JC: Oh dear.

D: But it got better in a couple of weeks.

JC: Mm.

D: Er ... when I were ... nine ... I started school before when I were eight. When I were nine I were in Mrs A _____'s class and it were good because I had two friends sitting on my table and they was always arguing to one another and going, 'I'm not your friend now', right, 'I'm not your friend now' and they ... and they were always like putting me off my work so I went to sit with Emma – she were on the same table – to see if it made any difference but ... but it didn't, they were always arguing.

D: Er ... now ... when I'm 16 I'm going to Canada but now it's ... er ... I'm in Mr N _____'s class now ... there's not much about now ... just normal.

JC: Mm. What's normal?

D: Oh yeah, I forgot ... My Auntie, she had a little baby called Stacie. She only had it last week ... and when ...

JC: When are you 16 then?

D: I'm going ... I might be going to Canada 'cos you know my ... 'cos my nanan, she had seven girls ... and they're all like ... they all want to go to ... other countries so soon ... when my auntie went to Canada she met this man and he asked her if she'd marry her and she said yes, so when ... so she's going to get married and when I'm 16 I want to go and see her in Canada. That's if my dad lets me. But she's going to pay for me to get there because ... my dad, he hasn't got a lot of money.

JC: Will you have left school when you are 16?

D: Um ... yeah. When I get back from Canada I'm going to study to be my job what I want to be. I want to be a doctor.

JC: Mm. What do you think you are going to have to do to be a doctor?

D: You have to study a long time, right, I were walking down the gennel with my friend and she told me what her job wanted to be and I told her what my job wanted to be. And she said: 'Oh God, you can't be a doctor because you've got to be so clever to be a doctor'. And I thought, well, if I pass all my exams and start studying I might be able to be a doctor.

JC: Mm.

D: And if not a doctor, a vet, and if not a vet a police lady.

JC: Mm.

D: Mm ... don't know ...

JC: So you think you're going to have to study quite hard, do you?

D: Mm.

JC: Are you looking forward to that?

D: My dad, he had to study a long time to be a painter and decorator.

JC: Mm.

D: And do you think that you're going to get married when you get older? What kind of family do you think you'll have?

D: Er ... don't know. My auntie, she had a boy and a girl so I might want a boy and a girl.

JC: Mm.

D: But my dad said not to get married until I'm about ... 29 ...

JC: Mm.

D: .... I can get my job first to be a doctor and then I can start my own family.

JC: Mm. Sounds very good. And where would you like to live?

D: Er ... well ... my dad's been to Worksop and he says it's all right – I want to live in England ...

JC: Mm.

D: Er ... I just might ... I'd like to live in a nice house ... and it might be in Sheffield. I want to live quite near to my dad ...

JC: Mm.

D: ... and my mum and my little sister.

JC: Mm. Going on to school now, which lesson do you like best? [Pause]

JC: Or more than one.

D: I like two. I like English ...

JC: Mm.

D: ... and I like maths.

JC: Mm.

D: ... but sometimes I'm not very good at maths. I like art and all, when we do them things. My dad says I'm good at art.

JC: Mm.

D: Like, at home we've got loads of paper what my nanan give us, 'cos she ... she has a load of paper, shopping lists even though she don't need it all and she gives ... she gives us half of it and I ... I drew like a robin on a branch and like ... things ... like ... you know nature ... background and trees and everything like that and I did that and my dad said it were good and he ... he's a good artist and all 'cos he can draw good rabbits and good robins and things. He has to copy it though. And I said to my dad, I wish I were like that boy that can go to a building and then he can go to somewhere else different and then he can do the building that he's seen.

JC: Mm.

D: I'm quite good at building.

JC: And which subjects don't you like so much? [Pause]

D: Um ... well I don't like it when like, you know when it's singing, I don't like it 'cos I can't sing very good. And ... er I don't ... I like them all really except for singing. Well I like singing but sometimes my voice goes a bit squeaky and I feel really embarrassed.

JC: Mm.

D: ... and I just, I like them all ...

JC: Mm.
      And what's your best subject? ... What are you best at doing at school?

D: Oh ... what am I best doing? ... [Pause]
      ... well, I'm good at English. My dad says I'm good at maths but sometimes I get hard ... I get stuck on some of these and I think I'm ... best at ... English but I'm not so good at anything else but I try my hardest but I think I'm best at English.

JC: Mm.

D: Like when ... I like it when you have to just do a story like ... when you've just been on six weeks' holiday and you have to do a story when you come back about what you've done and things like that and things like that. I think that's good.

JC: Is there anything you'd like to be better at?

D: Pardon?

JC: Is there anything you'd like to be better at?

D: Yeah. There ... I'd like to be better at ... I'd like to be better at
swimming. I'd like to be better at my maths and I'd like to be better
at ... topics because you know when Mr N _____ takes us to
the library and he says find something like out of books and everything you think 'Oh no, what can I do now?' And when like you
choose a subject on Turkey and you have to stay on that subject
and when you go to the country there's hardly any books about
Turkey and you think 'Oh no, let me think' ... er ... and my
auntie's best friend went to Turkey once and I know some things
about Turkey 'cos you know like their Turkish Delight ...

JC: Mm.

D: ... it's really, really, really sweet and I don't like it ...

JC: Mm.

D: ... and there's some Turkish houses are made out of rock like ...
like flintstones a bit and they ...

JC: Mm.

D: ... 'cos I've seen a photograph in a book about it.

JC: Mm. [Pause]

JC: Thank you very much. The next subject's about talking. Do you
think you are a talkative person?

D: Sometimes ... when somebody ... right if people just leave me
alone and let me do my work, I hardly ever talk then, I can get on
with it because I can't concentrate too much when people is talking
round me. But if anybody starts a conversation I can't stop having
a conversation because ...

JC: Mm.

D: ... 'cos when I get my head down and thinking about things, I
concentrate a lot but if somebody starts talking to me I just can't
do it at all, I can't think and things like that.

JC: So do you talk much in class?

D: Do I talk much in class? Well, sometimes I talk a lot ... when
Daniel starts messing about telling me jokes and everything; the
rest of the time I'm all right, I don't talk very much.

JC: Mm. [Pause]

JC: Who do you talk to in the class then? [Pause]

D: I talk to Massaret, I talk to Rhaksana when she's here, I talk to
Daniel, er I talk to Justina, I talk to nearly everybody in the class
...

JC: Mm.

D: ... but 'cos they're always coming to my table to borrow rubbers
and everything ...

221

JC: Mm.

D: ... so they upset [unclear] and things like that ...

JC: Mm. And what about talking to the teacher?

D: Er ... if I talk to the teacher a lot but when I'm stuck he has to help me ...

JC: Mm.

D: ... work and everything but most of the time he's ... he's like talking hisself like doing things on the board and things so you can't really talk to him when he is trying to learn children.

JC: Mm. Do you talk much at home?

D: Well, sometimes I talk when something's not very good on telly, but when 'Neighbours' is on I don't say a word ... [Laughter] ... and my sister, she does talk a lot ...

JC: Mm.

D: ... get fed up with it after a bit. And my dad is always saying 'Shush, shush'. [Laughter]

JC: Who do you talk to most then, do you think?

D: Mostly ... Justina, Mandy and Susie because we're always hanging around together and we always the best of friends and ... and it's like ... when ... when you're in the playground and there's nowt to do you ... you talk about things like what you've been doing last night and things like that and you talk about your best pop stars and everything. Justina and Mandy they are mad about 'The New Kids on the Block' and Susie she's mad about 'Big Fun'; I don't quite know who I'm mad about.

JC: Mm. And is there someone special that you talk to if you've got a problem or if you're worried about something?

D: My dad ...

JC: Mm.

D: ... but I never have any problems really, but if I'm worried about like my times table and everything, 'Dad will you test me on my times table please' and things like that and he helps me with my spelling and everything because he knows I'm not that good on spelling ...

JC: Mm.

D: ... and all things, he's like a teacher my dad really, when he's got the time. [Pause]

JC: Anything else you'd like to tell me about?

D: Um ... no.

JC: Now, Diana, would you describe yourself as a shy person?

D: Sometimes ...

JC: Mm.

D: ... if ... if like my cousin's come or something, first I'm shy, then get ... then get to start playing with him and that ...

JC: Mm.

D: ... like at first when you see somebody, you start being shy and then when you get to ... know them a bit more you start like playing with one another and things like that. I'm not shy all the time but ... if ... if like I go to an important thing I am shy.

JC: What's it like feeling shy?

D: Well, when you feel shy ... like if no-one's talking to you right, you think to yourself how am I going to start a conversation but you think really that they're shy an' all, that's why they don't talk to you ... but you feel shy because nobody's like talking to you an' everything and you don't like want to talk to them back ... and things like that.

JC: Mm. What do you do if you think you're going to feel shy? How do you overcome it?

D: Er ... I don't know really ... just try not to be shy and try to talk ... to get into a conversation and everything because my cousin he's not shy because if we like walked into their house he'd say 'Hi, how are you' and things like that.

JC: Mm. So what's the opposite of being shy, then?

D: Being talkative ...

JC: Mm.

D: ... like my sister ... er, probably not just sitting and being really shy just like try and relax and talk to them and things like that.

JC: Mm.
     Are there any times when you feel really confident and talkative?

D: Yeah. When I'm at my nanan's I do, when I'm at home I do and sometimes when I'm at my cousin's ...

JC: Mm.

D: ... when ... when she keeps ... I like it when she keeps talking on like so you can talk on with her to show people that you're not really shy. [Pause]

JC: Thank you.

Name Index

225

Subject Index